*From Making
a Profit to*

# MAKING A
# DIFFERENCE

*How to Launch Your New
Career in Nonprofits*

## Richard M. King

**PLANNING/COMMUNICATIONS**

River Forest, Illinois

**For quantity discounts and permissions, contact the publisher:**

**PLANNING/COMMUNICATIONS**

7215 Oak Avenue, River Forest, Illinois 60305
Phone: 708/366–5200
Internet URL: http://jobfindersonline.com

**Distribution to bookstores by:**
Midpoint Trade Books
212/727–0190

Cover design by Salvatore Concialdi
Front cover photograph copyright © 1999 by Comstock, Inc.

Produced using Corel Ventura Publisher 8.0

**Disclaimer of All Warranties and Liabilities**

**PUBLISHER'S CATALOGING–IN–PUBLICATION DATA**

*(Provided by Quality Books, Inc.)*

King, Richard M.
    From making a profit to making a difference:
how to launch your new career in nonprofits /
Richard M. King — 1st ed.

    p. cm.
    LCCN: 99–64177
    ISBN: 1–884587–17–8 (pbk.)
    ISBN: 1–884587–16–X (hbk.)

    1. Nonprofit organizations—Vocational guidance—United States.
2. Career changes.   I. Title.

HD2769.2.U6K56 2000           331.7'02
                      QBI99–1891

Business people who switch to a nonprofit career really are angels from heaven. But entering the nonprofit sector after a career in business can be a difficult and challenging journey.

In *From Making a Profit to Making a Difference*, author Richard M. King shows you how to overcome all the obstacles to successfully launch your new career in the nonprofit world.

"Rick King's counseling helped me make a successful transition from the corporate world to a nonprofit career. His advice in this book will **increase your chances for success in the nonprofit world.**"

> — *Win Hamilton, Executive Administrator, International Association of Lions Clubs*

"This book should become **a classic** reference for everyone in the for–profit world who wants to make a difference. Rick King takes you through an orderly process that is easy to follow and doesn't leave a stone unturned. At the same time, it provides you with in–depth insight into the nonprofit sector."

> — *Jack Bohlen, Vice–President of Philanthropy and Communication, Rush–Presbyterian–St. Luke's Medical Center*

**"Also useful to people already working for nonprofits** who are exploring career options, this book is filled with practical advice and lists of resources. I found King's insights on the similarities and differences between the sectors, his comments on how nonprofits work, and his advice on navigating a career transition to be most useful."

> — *Paul Lingenfelter, Vice President, The John D. and Catherine T. MacArthur Foundation*

**Other career books from Planning/Communications:**

- *Non–Profits & Education Job Finder*

- *Government Job Finder*

- *Professional's Job Finder*

- *National Job Hotline Directory:
  The Job Finder's Hot List*

- *Flight Attendant Job Finder & Career Guide*

- *International Job Finder: Where the Jobs are
  Worldwide* (available beginning August 2000)

# Table of Contents

Acknowledgments. . . . . . . . . . . . . . . . . . . . . . . . . . . . . iv

Preface. . . . . . . . . . . . . . . . . . . . . . . . . . . . . . . . . . . v

Why Foundations are a Bad Bet . . . . . . . . . . . . . . . . . . . . ix

1   **Assimilating Into the Nonprofit Culture.** . . . . . . . . . . . . 1

The New Nonprofit Environment. . . . . . . . . . . . . . . . . . . 2

Transition as Cultural Assimilation. . . . . . . . . . . . . . . . . 6

Culture Clash . . . . . . . . . . . . . . . . . . . . . . . . . . . . . 9

Preparing to Assimilate. . . . . . . . . . . . . . . . . . . . . . . 12

Two Real Life Examples . . . . . . . . . . . . . . . . . . . . . 13

2   **Transferring Business Skills to the Nonprofit Sector.** . . 21

Identifying Your Transferable Skills . . . . . . . . . . . . . . . . 25

Skills for the Nonprofit Sector . . . . . . . . . . . . . . . . . . 27

Study Findings . . . . . . . . . . . . . . . . . . . . . . . . . . . . 29

Case Study in Flexibility . . . . . . . . . . . . . . . . . . . . . . 33

Case Study in Resourcefulness . . . . . . . . . . . . . . . . . . 33

Case Study in Leadership . . . . . . . . . . . . . . . . . . . . . 34

3   **Classifying Your Nonprofit Interest** . . . . . . . . . . . . . . 36

Charitable Purposes and Causes. . . . . . . . . . . . . . . . . . 40

What Interests You?. . . . . . . . . . . . . . . . . . . . . . . . . . 45

Nonprofit Preference Indexing. . . . . . . . . . . . . . . . . . . 46

Nonprofit Preference Index . . . . . . . . . . . . . . . . . . . . 47

**4   Strategic Volunteerism. . . . . . . . . . . . . . . . . . . . . 62**

Strategic Volunteerism in Action . . . . . . . . . . . . . . . . 65

The Key Volunteer Role: Board of Directors . . . . . . . . . . 67

Finding the Board That's Right for You  . . . . . . . . . . . . 69

The Rubber Stamp Board. . . . . . . . . . . . . . . . . . . . . 70

The Participatory Board. . . . . . . . . . . . . . . . . . . . . . 71

The Corporate Board. . . . . . . . . . . . . . . . . . . . . . . . 72

Researching Organizational Boards . . . . . . . . . . . . . . . 74

Primary Information Sources. . . . . . . . . . . . . . . . . . . 75

Secondary Information Sources. . . . . . . . . . . . . . . . . 76

Adjunct Board Service Opportunities. . . . . . . . . . . . . . 77

United Way Loaned Executive Program  . . . . . . . . . . . . 79

**5   Networking In the Nonprofit Sector. . . . . . . . . . . . . . 81**

Making the Most of Your Business Contacts . . . . . . . . . . 82

Reaching the Nonprofit CEO . . . . . . . . . . . . . . . . . . . 85

Sources of Networking Information. . . . . . . . . . . . . . . 87

Annual Reports . . . . . . . . . . . . . . . . . . . . . . . . . . . 88

Membership Directories. . . . . . . . . . . . . . . . . . . . . . 89

Libraries . . . . . . . . . . . . . . . . . . . . . . . . . . . . . . . 90

Fund Raising Consulting Firms. . . . . . . . . . . . . . . . . . 91

Using the Internet . . . . . . . . . . . . . . . . . . . . . . . . . 92

Working with Search Consultants. . . . . . . . . . . . . . . . 93

**6   Resumes and Cover Letters for Nonprofit Jobs . . . . . . . 96**

The Resume Mystique. . . . . . . . . . . . . . . . . . . . . . . 97

The Problem with Business Resumes . . . . . . . . . . . . . . 98

The Nonprofit Resume Format. . . . . . . . . . . . . . . . . . 100

Educational Background . . . . . . . . . . . . . . . . . . . . . 103

Community Involvement . . . . . . . . . . . . . . . . . . . . . 105

Transferable Skills . . . . . . . . . . . . . . . . . . . . . . . . . . . 109

Business Brief. . . . . . . . . . . . . . . . . . . . . . . . . . . . . . . 113

Nonprofit References. . . . . . . . . . . . . . . . . . . . . . . . . . 115

The Cover Letter. . . . . . . . . . . . . . . . . . . . . . . . . . . . . 117

7 **Compensation In the Nonprofit Sector. . . . . . . . . . . . 126**

Business and Nonprofit Pay Standards Compared. . . . . . . 129

Determining the Value of Your Business Experience. . . . . . 132

Dealing With Irrelevant Experience . . . . . . . . . . . . . . . . 134

Understanding Salary Negotiations . . . . . . . . . . . . . . . . 136

Disclosing Your Current Salary. . . . . . . . . . . . . . . . . . . . 139

Two Exceptions . . . . . . . . . . . . . . . . . . . . . . . . . . . 140

8 **Directory of Nonprofit Recruiters . . . . . . . . . . . . . . . . 143**

Executive Search Firms Serving the Nonprofit Sector . . . . . 145

9 **Professional Fund Raising Consulting Firms. . . . . . . . . 152**

10 **Selected Professional Associations . . . . . . . . . . . . . . . 160**

11 **Sources of Philanthropic Information. . . . . . . . . . . . . . 165**

Foundation Center Cooperating Collections Network. . . . . 165

Organizations. . . . . . . . . . . . . . . . . . . . . . . . . . . . . . . 167

12 **Resource Collection . . . . . . . . . . . . . . . . . . . . . . . . . . 172**

How to Order . . . . . . . . . . . . . . . . . . . . . . . . . . . . . . . 173

Finding Job Vacancies. . . . . . . . . . . . . . . . . . . . . . . . . . 174

Resources for Nonprofit Careers . . . . . . . . . . . . . . . . . . 175

Changing Careers. . . . . . . . . . . . . . . . . . . . . . . . . . . . . 176

Applying for the Job. . . . . . . . . . . . . . . . . . . . . . . . . . . 176

**About the Author. . . . . . . . . . . . . . . . . . . . . . . . . . . . 178**

# Acknowledgments

I was encouraged to write this book by a variety of people who shared their common concerns and different experiences with me about the problems business executives encounter when launching a new career in the nonprofit sector. The directors of several Chicago–area foundations were concerned that the business professionals they had met who were serious about entering the nonprofit arena were "floating in limbo" on the nonprofit circuit without much direction or structure. Pete Henderson, former Executive Director of Chicago United, suggested that not every business professional is cut out to serve in a nonprofit management position. He suggested that somebody should develop a method for separating those who have great potential in the charitable sector from those who may not do well. Don Haider of the J.L. Kellogg Graduate School of Management at Northwestern University echoed that not enough specific information was available to business professionals to help them actually make a successful transition. Each, in a different way, influenced my decision to write this book.

Then there are the dozens of business professionals I have met with over the past few years, many of whom I have helped to find employment with nonprofit organizations. They shared with me their concerns, frustrations, fears, desires, road blocks, disappointments, and successes in making the transition. It is through their trials and errors that I have been able to identify the approaches to this transition that work and those that fail. I am grateful I had the opportunity to meet each of them and hope I was able to help each in some small way.

Richard M. King

# Preface

This book is written for the growing number of business professionals who are considering launching a new career in the nonprofit sector. The motivation to make this change may come early in your career when your path is little traveled and unknown, yet there is a desire to "do something that makes a difference." It may come in mid–career when your path is beginning to take shape but you yearn to "do something more meaningful." Or it may come near the end of your career after you have reached a number of professional and personal goals and want to "give back something to society." Whatever the reason or wherever the point is along your path, making the transition from the business world to the nonprofit sector can be one of the most rewarding adventures you will ever undertake. And it is likely to be the most challenging job search you will ever experience.

If this book can remove some of the considerable obstacles to making this transition, provide some insights into the nonprofit workplace, and give you some concrete ideas and techniques for making your business background relevant and competitive in the nonprofit sector, it will have achieved its purpose.

This is not just another "how–to" book. There are principles involved, but no patented formulas and no hype–laden promises of quick and easy results. In fact, the transition to nonprofit employment is as much a process as a result. It is a journey of discovery and learning in several dimensions, both professional and personal. It is an investment of considerable time and money. The success of your career transition is rooted in your acceptance of these realities.

The nonprofit sector is a diverse world within the broader service industry. Over 1.3 million organizations comprise the nonprofit sector. As the 20th century drew to a close, another 30,000 nonprofits were being created every year. Their purposes and activities are defined in terms of their organizational missions, not to be confused with a slogan or a trademark. The diversity of the nonprofit world makes it impossible to think of charitable organizations in generalities when it comes to considering employment opportunities. Professional associations are different from colleges, which differ from art museums, which are different from social service agencies. Although learning how specific nonprofit industries work will better prepare you to pursue employment opportunities in them, this understanding alone is just a very small element of the transition process.

You must begin the process of transition to the nonprofit sector by assessing your readiness, namely your potential for assimilating into the nonprofit culture. This concept of assimilation involves such things as your prior experiences with charities, your values, and your motives. How you have accomplished your goals, how you work with others, the manner in which you make business decisions, the level of adaptive and functional skills you have achieved — these are all linked to your readiness to work successfully in the nonprofit sector. Some people simply are not cut out to work for nonprofit organizations. Discovering this about yourself early on can save a lot of time and frustration.

The diverse nature of the nonprofit world provides an interesting patchwork of possibilities for employment. The most common roadblock for business professionals who want to switch to the charitable field is a lack of information about what the nonprofit world is all about. You probably already know just enough about the purposes or activities of a few nonprofit industries to identify those that interest you and those that don't. But how do you find meaningful work in nonprofits when there are so many different organizational missions to consider? Chapters 1 through 3 guide you through this challenge and help you through this maze.

Once you have evaluated your readiness and identified your nonprofit interests, you are ready to tackle transition strategies and tactics. Chapter 4 suggests some creative ways to position yourself for employment in the nonprofit sector. It demonstrates how you strategically use volunteer participation in charitable activities to build credentials in the nonprofit field while you are still working in the private sector, and how to plan your volunteer involvement with employment objectives in mind. The type of organization you select and the nature of the voluntary activities in which you engage are important strategic choices, ones which often can determine how short and how successful your transition process to nonprofit employment will be.

There is nothing like a network of personal contacts to open the doors to job opportunities. In your business career you build a network of these contacts every day, networks likely to expand the longer you remain in a line of work. But these networks are in the private sector. It's likely that you haven't made nearly as many contacts in the nonprofit world. But since most people find new jobs through their personal network, the lack of a nonprofit network poses a major problem for launching a new career in nonprofits. Fortunately, there are a lot of nonprofit professionals out there ready to help you. You just have to know who they are and how to connect with them. Chapter 5 will show you how.

Chapter 6 is devoted to preparing your resume and cover letters. Changing careers even within the business sector often requires a whole new language and understanding. So it is in the nonprofit universe. Many terms and jargon, acronyms, industry buzz words, and hot buttons that you use daily in the business world are probably going to be meaningless to the hiring executive at a nonprofit organization. Thus, if the language you use in your resume is unfamiliar or mismatched, if an employer does not understand the relevance of your accomplishments to its nonprofit setting, how can she figure out where you fit in her organization? These are very real obstacles to transition that you can avoid by presenting your background and qualifications in a manner you would never use in the business world. Be prepared to rethink your business accomplishments in a way that will create a completely different resume format and cover letter approach for your job search in the nonprofit jungle!

Compensation in the nonprofit sector is often a perplexing transition factor. It's no secret that people employed in the nonprofit world generally earn less than their counterparts in the business sector. However, compensation in the nonprofit world is a very mixed bag based on many industry variables. Salary ranges run the gamut depending on the type of nonprofit entity. Should you expect to take a salary cut — and how much of a cut, if any — when making the transition to nonprofit employment? How do you equate the value of your business experience with the nature of a specific nonprofit job? How much can you negotiate your initial salary and benefits? Chapter 7 answers these questions and many more.

Chapters 8 through 12 provide directories of resources that will facilitate your transition to the nonprofit world. The directory of firms that recruit executives for nonprofits presented in Chapter 8 helps you find the recruiters who can help your new job search. Chapters 9 and 10, respectively, present a directory of selected consulting firms that conduct fund raising and a directory of selected professional associations that illustrate the breadth of opportunities in association management. Chapter 11 furnishes details on where to find information about charitable organizations while Chapter 12 provides a collection of resources that will help you find a job in nonprofits and facilitate the launch of your new career.

## WHY FOUNDATIONS ARE A BAD BET

You may have noticed that I've been ignoring a large part of the nonprofit universe: foundations. Foundations are a significant part of the American philanthropic heritage. They perform important work by identifying and supporting charitable activities here and abroad. *But foundations rarely offer job opportunities for professionals just leaving the business world.* Consequently, I have not included private foundations as a part of the nonprofit job transition.

First, foundation jobs are difficult to obtain because so few of them are available and they tend to turn over very slowly. Foundation executives are a close–knit group. Foundations as an industry segment, especially the larger ones, tend to be highly selective and somewhat insular in their hiring practices. Corporate foundations often are managed by the company's public affairs officer. Grant administration often is accomplished through the public affairs office without the need for additional management–level staff.

With the exception of a relatively few foundations that actually run their own programs, foundations are not public charities and therefore do not operate programs nor engage in direct service delivery activities. Job responsibilities at the program management level in foundations usually are limited to particular grants, planning, and processing functions. Unlike public charities there is generally a lack of job variety in all but the largest foundations, which can result in a less stimulating environment and narrowly–defined job responsibilities. The business professional seeking to launch a new career in nonprofits is unlikely to find a job with a foundation — so I've left foundations out of the mix in this book. If you still want to try to find work with a foundation, see the *Non–Profits & Education Job Finder* discussed on page 174.

One word of caution before you forge ahead. Reading this book may result in finding a purpose in your work life more fulfilling than you have ever imagined. If you're ready to face that possibility, let's begin.

Richard M. King

Chapter

1

# Assimilating Into the Nonprofit Culture

During my early days as an executive recruiter for nonprofit organizations and institutions, I rarely came upon business executives interested in working for nonprofit organizations. All they wanted was to make a profit, not a difference. The nonprofit world was something of an anomaly to them, resting somewhere between the two major sectors of the working world: private enterprise (corporate) and public service (government). To business professionals, nonprofits really were an alien "Third Sector," a separate world that had a hard time interacting with the other two.

Consequently, business professionals seldom thought of nonprofit organizations as a field with employment opportunities for them. Back in the early 1970s, there were far fewer nonprofit organizations than today. "Charitable" causes like conserving natural resources were not yet sufficiently etched into the public consciousness for business professionals to leave their lucrative private sector careers and actually work toward making a difference. The business and nonprofit sectors represented two distinctly different career paths without many opportunities to cross over.

But the career world has changed a lot during the past ten years. More business professionals than ever are seeking jobs in the nonprofit sector, and more charitable organizations are hiring them. Over 1.3 million nonprofits in the United States, with more than 8 million employees and 80 million volunteers now comprise the "Third Sector" of the U.S. economy. Over 30,000 new charities are formed each year. In addition to their paid employees, nonprofits reap the fruits of free labor: 56 percent of the U.S. adult population donates an average of 4.3 hours per person of volunteer service every week. Add in these volunteers, and nonprofits constitute America's largest employers. The nonprofit, or charitable sector, has always been a "growth industry," but only recently has its expansion begun to create extensive career opportunities for business professionals.

# THE NEW NONPROFIT ENVIRONMENT

As those aging Baby Boomers redefine the concept of multiple careers, an increasing number of them — as well as recent college graduates — are fleeing the profit-driven world to apply their skills in the nonprofit com-

**SYLVIA**

munity to help make a real difference in our nation's welfare. With the sad spectacle of consolidation and mega–mergers that produce massive layoffs, today's workers lack the job security the private sector offered the Depression Era generation. Not only are "Boomers" open to moving on to two or three different career tracks during their work life, many actively plan that strategy. While advances in technology have created many of these new career opportunities, Boomers are including nonprofit opportunities in their multiple career scenarios as well. Even if only a small percentage of the 75 million Boomers born between 1946 and 1964 make the transition from business to nonprofit work, their sheer numbers alone would have a significant impact on the workplace.

Today's migration to nonprofits also results from the values and environment in which Boomers grew up that compliment the values of the nonprofit culture. People raised in the era of Dr. Spock and who came of age during the Kennedy years, the struggle for basic civil rights, the Vietnam War, and Watergate were largely idealistic, progressive advocates for social change. Wanting to create a better society, they were imbued with a sense of independence. They were better educated than their parents and grandparents, and were committed to their beliefs. This value system is fundamental to the career and lifestyle choices Boomers have made. And it is a value system that is shared throughout the nonprofit sector. This commonality makes the transition of the business professional to the nonprofit sector much more likely than a generation ago. But it is only one reason for the new nonprofit environment.

The 1990s represent one of the longest, most active thriving economic climates in U.S. history. This prosperity also has had an enormous trickle–down effect on the financial good fortune of charitable organizations. As nonprofits have been able to expand their programs they have also had to increase their paid staff. As many charitable groups have become a big business themselves, their leaders have begun to realize that they need employees with skills common to the business world. As nonprofits have grown, their leaders have started hiring accountants, financial managers, media–savvy public relations experts, solid business managers, information managers, marketers, information technology wizards, planners, and other traditionally private sector professionals.

> **Solid business skills have become more valuable to nonprofits as they diversify their activities in a more aggressive manner.**

Solid business skills have become more valuable to nonprofits as they diversify their activities in a more aggressive manner. Charities have became more business–like, much to the pleasure of the philanthropic community as well as the corporations that often have berated nonprofits for their apparently lax controls over their operations. This new direction has translated into new job opportunities where business skills are highly valued.

For example, in the early 1980s, leaders of the health care industry realized that restructuring the traditional hospital operation into a multi–corporate system was essential to keeping the industry one step ahead of government regulations that would cut into the health care industry's healthy profit margins. They discovered the value of marketing as they realized that consumerism and managed care competition in health care eventually would require them to adopt a whole new strategy. By the mid–1980s health care systems were hiring corporate marketing executives with consumer product backgrounds and the entire health care industry began competing on an entirely new level.

Current social problems have helped fuel this movement to bring business professionals into the nonprofit sector. The growth of the environmental movement over the past few decades has made worldwide conservation not only politically acceptable, but also a multi–national priority supported by both the public and private sectors. Issues of poverty, affordable housing, unemployment, gang violence, drug abuse, hunger, homelessness, and healthcare are continuing problems the media chronicles on a daily basis. The growing ability of nonprofits to attract attention to their causes and to pull in business professionals as volunteers and contributors has also given business professionals a closer look at the possibilities for employment with nonprofits.

Despite all of this movement, leaving a career in business for a job with a nonprofit organization is still quite a challenging leap. The fact that more business professionals than ever are seeking jobs in the charitable industry in no way implies that the nonprofit job market is ready for, or can immediately absorb all of them. This book should give you an edge over other business professionals who also wish to enter the nonprofit universe.

Today we are on the forefront of a slow moving wave of change in the nonprofit industry where the identification and selection of business professionals to fill jobs traditionally held by nonprofit career professionals is slowly becoming common, and business professionals are beginning to move smoothly between jobs in the private and non–profit sectors. Until we reach the point where business people are fully accepted in the non-profit world, you will need to use the unique job–search strategies and tactics suggested in this book to successfully make the transition to working for nonprofit organizations.

## TRANSITION AS CULTURAL ASSIMILATION

The first step is recognizing that the switch from the profit–oriented world of business to nonprofits is a major change in "corporate" cultures. To get some idea of the sort of cultural transition you will face when moving to a nonprofit, recall the film "Dances With Wolves." The movie depicted the story of a young Civil War officer who chooses to single–handedly man an isolated outpost in Oglala Sioux territory. He slowly befriends the Sioux tribe and eventually becomes "one of them" through a fascinating process of cultural assimilation. While the nonprofit industry as a whole has grown tremendously over the years, it still is regarded by many as unknown territory, a different culture, the mysterious and misunderstood "Third Sector" of the economy. In many ways the transition from a business career to a non–profit career is like a process of cultural assimilation. It requires an acceptance of different values, different norms and structures, and even a different language.

Thinking of your transition to the non–profit work place as a process similar to cultural assimilation provides a helpful framework as you begin to think about your interest in working for a nonprofit organization. Assimilating from one culture to another consists of certain elements that parallel the process of transition from the private sector to the nonprofit sector. Learning about a new culture requires you to study its norms, language, values, organizing principles, and customs. It is difficult to live in a new culture unless you first study it and understand how it works. This takes time. There is much to learn and we can absorb only so much at one time.

> **A NOTE ON LANGUAGE**
>
> The terms "nonprofit" and "charitable organization" are used interchangeably throughout this book.
>
> Rather than use the awkward "he/she" construct that gets in the way of clear writing, my publisher's policy is to alternate the gender of pronouns.

It takes time to make the transition from business to nonprofit employment for the same reasons. This is not like changing jobs within your career path, where the accumulation of skills and experience you have are simply applied at a higher level or in a position of wider managerial scope. To be realistic, you must be willing to accept that the transition process may take a long time for you to achieve. This is not to say that you cannot do it in a relatively short period of time. Some business professionals have found jobs with nonprofits in a matter of months, usually with favorable extenuating circumstances and a lot of luck. They are the exceptions. More typically you will find that the more effort you put into preparing yourself, learning and experiencing the nonprofit sector, and applying the techniques presented in this book, the more likely it is that your transition will be more rapid and more rewarding.

Cultures are "people," not "things." Understanding how people of a different culture think, what they believe, why they do things a certain way, what they value, where they are at risk, how they interact with each other and with outsiders — one assimilates these things only by interacting with the people of that culture, by being among them. The same is true in the nonprofit world. And the nonprofit world offers a method of interaction that is unique: volunteerism. Having an opportunity to work with the staff of a charitable organization is an experience afforded many business professionals as volunteers, either as members of the board of directors or in a more hands on, direct service capacity, whether it be stuffing envelopes, running a marathon, writing a brochure, or managing other volunteers. Chapter 4 examines how to strategically use volunteerism to ease your transition to the nonprofit sector and find job opportunities. This kind of affiliation also provides opportunities for networking, an important part of any job search, and a job–search technique covered in depth in Chapter 5.

Having studied and learned about a new culture and having lived among the "natives" to see what they are all about, the assimilation process is not complete and successful unless you learn the specific skills required to survive in that new cultural environment. The tools you

have used in your old world may not work in the new culture. Availability of resources may be quite different and the manner in which people work together, in part due to the nature of resources at their disposal, may require that you develop new skills. The financial and human resources customarily available in the business world are rarely available to nonprofits. Stewardship of resources becomes an important management strategy as well as a measure of accountability for executive leadership. This final adjustment in the development of survival skills is often the most difficult for business professionals to make.

# CULTURE CLASH

The business world and the nonprofit world can be characterized as clash of different cultures. These differences are substantial and begin with the most basic elements. While the business sector's primary goal is to make a profit for shareholders through the sale of goods and services, nonprofits strive to be agents of change: building affordable housing, a child learning, appreciating art, building community, saving a child from the streets, enjoying a clean environment.

> Unlike the business world, the process of how decisions are made in nonprofits is often as important as the decision itself.

The business sector raises capital through the sale of stock and manages its financial affairs with a close eye on reducing tax liabilities. The nonprofit sector raises capital by soliciting charitable gifts from individuals, corporations, foundations, and government sources. It manages its financial affairs with a close eye on personnel costs. The business sector talks about return on investment, debt–equity ratios, marginal utility, and governmental interference. The nonprofit sector talks about sources of funding support, constituency building, volunteer recruitment, and balanced budgets.

Business professionals who have made the transition to the nonprofit sector agree that the "process orientation" of the nonprofit culture is the single most significant factor in assimilation. The most obvious manifestation of this process orientation is the slower decision-making procedures of nonprofits compared to the business world. Unlike the business world, the process of how decisions are made in nonprofits is often as important as the decision itself. Sometimes the process of making the decision is even more important than the decision because the process, in terms of internal politics, serves a distinct purpose within the organization's dynamic. Experienced non–profit executives are oriented to an understanding of the importance of process within this culture.

The majority of business professionals are, on the other hand, outcome oriented. The business culture rewards quick decision making, especially when it leads to profits. Establishing a process of decision making that runs counter to timely reaction and response is not only costly to a business venture, but also culturally verboten. Consequently, adjusting to the centrality of process orientation in the nonprofit world can be difficult for business professionals. Assimilating into a culture where the emphasis is on process rather than profit can be a huge barrier for many business people making the transition to the non–profit world. Some find it merely frustrating and perplexing; many others never adapt to it. Others try to cope with it and fail. So, why is the process orientation so central to the nonprofit culture, and why is it so crucial for business professionals to assimilate it?

The most pervasive reason for process orientation is the presence of multiple constituent groups which accompany every non–profit entity. Unlike business where constituent groups share the same motive, namely maximizing profits, nonprofit constituent groups are likely to have a variety of motives and points of view — even when they generally support and agree with the mission of the organization. While a belief in profit is universal and straightforward, a belief in altruism can take on many shades. Internally, an interdisciplinary employee group creates a need for process orientation.

Just about any university offers a good illustration. Its "internal" constituent groups include its board of directors, faculty, and students, plus building engineering, finance and accounting, development, publishing, and legal departments, among others. Faculty alone is comprised of many different disciplines. Many disciplines are represented; many points of view exist.

This same school's external constituents include alumni, friends, community and neighborhood residents, donors, plus governmental officials and regulatory agencies. Many viewpoints exist here as well. Successful university administrators figure out a way to provide a process for input and participation by all these differing constituent groups while retaining management and leadership authority. Without incorporating process orientation in running the institution, one of the constituent groups most certainly would step in and take over.

Another reason for the importance of process orientation is reverence for the cultural value that might be called "getting along." The ability of employees to work together is crucial in nonprofit organizations. So it is with members of the board of directors and key volunteers as well. Working in harmony with each other requires that all points of view be considered, that full disclosure and discussion be afforded to all, and that people be treated with respect and dignity even if dissenting views are expressed. Beyond this, people who share the same passion for the work of the nonprofit organization expect to be involved and included in its work. Thus, the group expects a process orientation as a way of continually articulating the direction of the organization through an inclusive style of communication.

## PREPARING TO ASSIMILATE

Some people have a greater propensity to successfully assimilate the nonprofit culture than others. The most significant factor related to one's capacity to assimilate is a very simple one to understand: preparation. To demonstrate this need for preparation, and to introduce many of the key transition strategies presented in this book, consider the following two case examples of Bill and Donna which illustrate the effect that preparation has on whether or not you'll successfully make the switch into the nonprofit community.

## Two Real Life Examples

### Bill: From Seed Business to Nonprofit Executive

Bill was a successful 42–year old business entrepreneur who had taken over his family's wholesale seed company ten years earlier. An avid downhill skier, sports enthusiast, and college all–star basketball player, he started thinking more seriously about the idea of running a non–profit organization, something he had pondered the past year or so. He was in my office to begin to explore that possibility.

"Over the past ten years I've transformed a fledgling mom and pop business into a very profitable and competitive enterprise," he said. "But what I really want to do now is take those business skills I've perfected and apply them to a leadership role in a nonprofit organization. I really think that most charities lack the business orientation to operate more effectively and I think I can make a real contribution in this regard."

Bill had no particular nonprofit setting in mind and admitted that he was not knowledgeable enough about the industry to have any preferences, except that he would not consider running an organization that was very small. He said that compensation was not a factor. He had income from investments and other holdings which would continue to provide him with a good income stream even if he left the seed company today. He believed that his financial situation would be attractive to a charity when it came to determining salary.

Further discussion with Bill revealed that he had rarely done volunteer work for any nonprofit organizations. He had been an officer for the regional chapter of a seed industry association, but that was about it. A former college classmate who was now the provost of a major Eastern university was the only person Bill knew in the nonprofit sector. He could recall no family members or friends who had ever worked in the nonprofit sector. He described his greatest strengths as turning a stagnant, unprofitable business into a going concern, creative deal-making, and being an expert in the wholesale seed business.

> **The classic entrepreneurial personality type is often ill–suited for the leadership needs of a nonprofit organization.**

When our meeting ended, I had to tell Bill something I knew he did not want to hear: it would take a considerable amount of time for him to make a successful transition into the kind of nonprofit leadership opportunity he sought. "The market is that bad?" he replied. "No," I said. " simply not prepared to make the transition." I proceeded to explain the many factors that led me to that conclusion. Bill's interest in seeking a nonprofit leadership position was predicated on a negative, namely that nonprofit organizations lack the business acumen to run effectively. As motives go, that's pretty thin.

There is no question that knowledge and experience in financial management, accounting, personnel, budgeting, planning and administration are necessary executive abilities for running a nonprofit organization. But if it were a simple matter of applying business skills to nonprofits, every business executive in the world would be qualified to direct a charitable organization. There's just more to it than that. After Bill brings his considerable business skills to the organization, what happens next? I did not get a sense from him that the mission and direction of a charity was compelling to him. Somehow, he would have to learn this before he could consider himself competitive in his search for nonprofit leadership.

Another telling factor was Bill's work style. He was obviously a successful entrepreneur: a hard driven, quick acting decision maker with great intuitive business sense and an incredible feel for the numbers — all the qualities required to run a business in the highly competitive business environment.

The problem was that the classical entrepreneurial personality type is often not suitable for nonprofit organization leadership needs. The entrepreneur generally tends to make decisions independently, rarely consulting others before taking action. Many manage people poorly and do not delegate tasks well because they don't take the time for these activities. Bill would probably be quite frustrated by the "corporate culture" in nonprofits. His entrepreneurial style and the nonprofit culture almost certainly would clash. He would have to learn more about the management dynamics and leadership requirements of nonprofits before he could make a successful transition.

Bill's lack of experience as a volunteer with charitable organizations also concerned me as did his lack of personal contacts in the nonprofit community. From a networking standpoint, he would be starting from ground zero. In addition, the way he reported his personal financial situation and the compensation he might seek from a nonprofit was very revealing. There is no question that nonprofits are conscious of personnel expenditures (in some organizations, personnel costs are as much as 90 percent of total expenses). But most nonprofits acknowledge that they have to pay a competitive salary to attract and retain qualified executive leadership. Although well–intentioned, Bill's attitude about compensation would create skepticism about his intentions on the part of any legitimate organization. Before any potential nonprofit employer would take him seriously, Bill would have to use a resource like the *Non–Profits & Education Job Finder* (see page 174 for details) to identify salary surveys that would tell him how much people with his experience and education are paid for the types of positions he is seeking. See Chapter 7 for a thorough discussion of compensation practices among nonprofits.

Finally, the fact that Bill had been a chief executive officer of a business for the past ten years does not automatically make him qualified to serve as a chief executive for a nonprofit entity. At that level, boards of directors usually require content–specific skills and experience in their chief executive officer. Bill probably would be competing with nonprofit executives who have the relevant content–specific backgrounds. He would fare poorly against such serious competition.

## Donna: Viewing Herself Too Narrowly

When I met her, Donna was a single, 35 year–old woman who working as an account manager for a medium–sized brokerage firm in Chicago. She was a *cum laude* graduate of Michigan State University's business school. Her petite frame and easy manner belied her considerable success in developing new investment business for her firm. In four of the seven years she had been with the company she led all other account managers in new business development. She had purchased a three–flat on Chicago's Gold Coast. Proud of her accomplishments, and financially comfortable, she was in my office to talk about changing careers to the non–profit sector.

"I'm just tired of squeezing out another one–quarter point for greedy customers," she said. "I look around at what's happening in this country, the homeless that live under Wacker Drive, children abused for just being children. I don't feel very productive anymore. There's something missing. I know I can't change the world but I know I can do something."

She was not the first person to wish to put relevance and meaning into her work, to feel that she is contributing to a greater good. Nor was she the first person to get stuck right there. "The problem is, I don't know much about nonprofits except that they can't make a profit" — a statement that only proved her point. "I've been selling investments for the past five years. I doubt that this is something nonprofits are looking for." She was right, of course, but she was looking at herself too narrowly.

When I asked her to describe the most outstanding skills she had developed over the past several years, she narrowed them down two major achievements:

☐ The successful way she related to her client investors, insightfully noting her effectiveness in a male–dominated industry, and

☐  A high level of intuitive judgment when it came to data.

It was clear that Donna had a good understanding of herself. She was achievement oriented, liked to juggle a lot of agendas, was highly self-directed — but not in a selfish way — and she had a very outgoing personality.

Donna sat on the board of directors of a homeless shelter for the last five years, something to which a former college friend had introduced her. She had served as an officer for three years, and chaired the long–range planning committee as well. That led to some other volunteer work she pursued with the Special Olympics for young adults with developmental disabilities. Through her company she was selected to serve on a United Way task force to study the effects of different allocation formulas on investment policies. It became clear that these experiences provided Donna with a solid understanding of the nonprofit environment. She had not yet developed her network of contacts, but her volunteer involvement had set the stage for building and exploiting it.

Two months later a national network of food bank depositories headquartered in Chicago was seeking a national distribution manager. The executive director of the homeless shelter where Donna served on the board regularly received food from a local food bank. He had heard about the opening from its director. He told Donna about the position after a board meeting and offered to introduce her. The job involved coordinating food supplies donated by hundreds of food manufacturers around the country via a rail and trucking system. The donated food would eventually end up in shelters, social service programs, and church pantries for distribution to the needy. It required continuous communication with major food producers and distributors. The distribution manager was in a pivotal position on the organization's management chart.

Donna's accomplishments were obviously an important component in meeting the requirements for this job. But just as important was the relevance of the organization's mission to Donna's accomplishments. This nonprofit needed a gutsy, business–disciplined, people-oriented professional to run a complicated distribution system. It needed someone who was not intimidated by male organizational bias nor afraid to make quick, independent decisions. Its mission was driven by a need to get donated food quickly and safely into the mouths of the needy in a cost–effective and efficient manner.

The organization interviewed Donna several times. It turned out that the group was more interested in her volunteer leadership background at the homeless shelter and at the United Way than in her accomplishments in the investment field. In the end, the network selected her for the job over several candidates who had worked for nonprofit organizations. It was clear that the organization did not base its hiring decision on her sales background at the investment firm. That job was not relevant to the group's needs as an organization, nor to the national distribution manager's duties. Donna's volunteer experience enabled her to overcome the initial hurdle and launch her new career — and assimilation — into the nonprofit world.

Successful assimilation into the nonprofit community — so necessary to the transition from the private sector to nonprofits — consists of a number of steps that are detailed in the rest of this book. Chapter 2 explains "skills transference" — which business skills meet the needs of nonprofit positions — and helps you chart your skills. Chapter 3 includes a unique "Nonprofit Preference Index" that will help you classify your interests so you can decide what sort of nonprofit work will be most rewarding. Chapter 4 shows how to use "Strategic Volunteerism" to enhance your prospects of winning the nonprofit jobs that really appeal to you. Chapter 5 equips you for building and using a network of contacts in the nonprofit community to find job openings and get hired. Chapter 6 offers guidelines and examples for writing an effective resume and cover letter than will get you interviewed even if you have no experience in nonprofits. Chapter 7 explores salary and benefits issues with tips for effective salary negotiation. The remaining chapters include a directory of executive recruiters for nonprofits, a directory of professional fund raising consulting firms, a directory of selected professional associations, sources of philanthropic information including the Foundation Center's "Cooperating Collections Network," and a resource collection of career books and software useful for your job quest.

# Transferring Business Skills to the Nonprofit Sector

Some people define their workplace skills far too narrowly. For example, Mary was a 37 year–old marketing manager for a community bank that a financial services holding company recently acquired. The "reduction in force" that cost Mary her job offered a good severance package and outplacement assistance.

At this point in her career, Mary really wanted to work for a nonprofit organization. When I met with Mary for the first time, I asked her to tell me about her most highly developed work skills.

"Since I have always been in marketing, first for a transportation company, then for a metals manufacturer, and then for a bank, I think marketing is my strong suit," she replied. Anything else, I asked? "No, that's about it. I've always had a marketing title. I don't think I'm qualified to do much else."

During her 15 years in marketing, Mary developed a rich array of skills she could transfer to another type of job in the private or nonprofit sector. But as long as she defined herself in terms of her job title she would never recognize her transferable skills. Like Mary, the longer you work, the more likely you are to perceive your skills very narrowly, while, in reality, your skills have usually grown and expanded.

In a 1967 presentation to the American Psychological Association entitled *Nature of Skills: Implications for Education and Training,* Sidney Fine shared his findings on how personal skills relate to career development. His conclusions are very relevant to the process of job transition from the business to the nonprofit sector. In reality, most of the skills that are valued in the workplace are valuable in a broad array of careers. For example, being highly organized is a deftness that carries great value whether you work in the business world, for government, or a nonprofit organization. Being a "conscientious worker" is a workplace attribute that is so highly and widely valued that it is now expected of all employees. It is not surprising that the most valued skills in the workplace are also highly transferable from job to job as well as from one employment sector to another.

Fine identified three categories of skills to illustrate how various personal abilities are useable in career development:

**Adaptive skills** are capabilities that involve your behavior in the workplace, personality characteristics, mannerisms, and ways of doing things. They are skills you learned early in life to cope with and react to your environment. They are skills that you are still developing so you can adjust to and accept the things around you. Adaptive skills determine how you "fit" in certain organizational settings. They are relational in nature. If you are a very punctual person, you will really stand out in an organizational setting that does not value punctuality. How you treat coworkers, the manner in which you dress, the way you react to stress, how you relate to your boss, your attitude about work, your influence on the people around you — these are all adaptive skills that all of us have developed and use daily.

 **Functional skills** include analyzing data, negotiating contracts, planning schedules, investigating problems, preparing budgets, evaluating programs, interpreting information, corresponding with customers, checking for quality, and mediating disagreements — all of which are general competencies that enable you to relate the data, people, and things that make up the workplace. A "job description" depicts the combination of different functional skills required to perform a particular work assignment. Certain jobs require using a standard set of functional skills. For example, an internal auditor must use a set of specific functional skills to perform her job. Most managerial positions require many related functional skills which we use nearly every day.

**Content–specific skills** are the competencies that fulfill the technical requirements of a specific job, according to specific standards. You are not born with these skills, nor are they readily or easily acquired. You generally develop these skills through formal academic or technical training as well as on–the–job internships and continuing education. Content–specific skills are required for most professional positions such as medicine and law as well as law enforcement, architecture, engineering, personnel administration, and commodities brokering.

While adaptive and functional skills are highly transferable, content–specific language often obscures them. For example, marketing encompasses a broad spectrum of specific job activities and an even broader range of skills. Personal selling, advertising, promotion, public relations and consumer research are some of the different aspects of marketing. But when you think of marketing, you rarely think of the functional and adaptive skills a marketer possesses. Instead you think of those technical content–specific skills a marketer applies on the job.

For example, consider the sales manager at a clothing store. To succeed in her job, it is pretty obvious that the sales manager uses her:

1    Adaptive skills such as an outgoing personality, persistence, persuasiveness, charm, and energy;

2    Functional skills including managing and motivating staff, calculating numerical data, collecting money, utilizing information systems, handling customer complaints; and

3    Content–specific skills such as merchandising, pricing, buying, inventory control, and retail advertising.

Her adaptive and functional skills are readily transferable to many other jobs, but her content–specific skills are more limited to the retail sales industry.

# IDENTIFYING YOUR TRANSFERABLE SKILLS

Most people typically think of their jobs in content–specific terms. Such a mind set can get in your way when you consider shifting your career to the nonprofit world because content–specific skills are usually very hard to transfer to other jobs.

Consequently, it is critical that you take enough time to identify your most transferable capabilities: your adaptive and functional skills. This is a difficult assignment for most of us. It's not inspirational. It may seem to be an elementary exercise, much like something your college career counselor might have had you do. *But the importance of this skills identification process will become clearer as you learn more about the nonprofit sector.*

When you first begin to consider your skills, your descriptions probably will be fairly superficial and slanted by labels and business jargon. Don't worry if you make several attempts at this before you put together a meaningful compilation of skills. Once you have a short list of those skills documented, put it aside for a day. Return to this task every day for a week or so. At work, make a conscious attempt to identify the functional and adaptive skills you use at the office every day. Jot them down immediately so you don't forget them. A close and trusted co–worker can help you confirm the skills you identify. Does she see your skills the same way you do? How would she describe your skills?

You should develop your own terms and language to describe your capabilities. To help get you started, check out the following list of typical skills. Use an action word — a verb, or variation thereof — as the first word for each of your skills that you identify.

## TYPICAL BUSINESS SKILLS

- Appraising programs
- Analyzing reports
- Auditing fiscal information
- Advising staff
- Buying outside services
- Budgeting revenue and expense
- Building external relationships
- Compiling complicated information
- Coordinating the work of others
- Creating new procedures
- Delegating responsibilities
- Distributing information
- Editing documents for publication
- Evaluation program effectiveness
- Initiating projects
- Investigating problem areas
- Mediating conflicts
- Monitoring program efforts
- Negotiating contractual services
- Organizing major events
- Planning for short term goals
- Planning for long range goals
- Programming computer information
- Recruiting people for hiring
- Researching critical information
- Speaking in public
- Supervising others
- Writing creatively

# SKILLS FOR THE NONPROFIT SECTOR

In 1989 the National Assembly of National Voluntary Health and Social Welfare Organizations examined the issue of effective community leadership. Working with the United Way national office, Dr. Jim Goodrich, a professor of management at the University of the Pacific, and John Shaw, an IBM executive on loan to the project, surveyed and interviewed 270 human service organization managers, who had been identified as outstanding in their field, as well as selected directors of their organizations.

The study sought to determine the most important characteristics managers need to effectively lead nonprofit organizations. Their final conclusions identified the following five key attributes.

 ### Adaptability

Initial data from the interviews indicated that the effective manager has an unusual command of all four leadership styles: directing, guiding, supporting, and delegating. The nonprofit human service sector requires adaptability because of the different constituencies to which the manager must relate and the variety of functions she must supervise.

 ### Concern for People

Staff and board members alike often described the better human service managers as "caring" and "empathetic." They achieved organizational goals by emphasizing empowering staff, volunteers, and their board of directors rather than excessively monitoring and controlling their actions.

## Dealing with Change

Effective managers were able to maintain a balance between openness to change and focusing on their organization's original mission. In every nonprofit, the needs of various constituencies change for several reasons, such as an influx of new populations, shifting social conditions, and changes in the law. Effective managers are able to anticipate these changes and make appropriate alterations in programming, resource allocation, and develop new service areas while still adhering to the integrity of their organization's mission.

## Demonstrating Autonomy

The best managers personify leadership in the agency. They effectively *become* the agency in the eyes of its employees and the community. This means being able to establish personal credibility as someone whose words are supported by action, coupled with personal involvement and a perception that the manager has things well in hand.

## Commitment to Key Values

One of the highest–rated scales in the study was understanding and exemplifying the organization's key values. An ability to internalize the nonprofit organization's values and mission may be what separates the effective nonprofit manager from all the rest, including corporate managers.

Other researchers have corroborated the Goodrich and Shaw findings. Investigators for the Center for Creative Leadership, Cynthia McCauley and Martha Hughes, asked managers in both the business nonprofit sectors to identify the skills and qualities they felt were most important to succeed in their positions. Both groups were given 16 qualities from which they were to select the eight they believed were most important. The results of this study surprised more than a few investigators.

Before I reveal their findings, it would be worthwhile to rank these characteristics yourself — so don't peek at their findings below yet. All of these 16 qualities are important characteristics for managers to possess. This exercise asks you to select the eight qualities that you consider to be the most important for managerial success. So go to the next page and rank them from one through eight, with one being the most important of all.

## STUDY FINDINGS

 **Before reading any further, be sure to complete the exercise on the next page that was described immediately above.**

This study found that the business and nonprofit sectors are more alike than you might intuitively expect. Although the cultures of the business and the nonprofit sector are quite different, they share a surprisingly close set of values when it comes to the management qualities they respect the most. McCauley and Hughes found that corporate *and* nonprofit managers selected the same three qualities as the most important: flexibility, resourcefulness, and leading staff. On a percentage basis, the two groups also ranked five of the top six qualities nearly exactly the same: flexibility (three point differ-

# RANK EIGHT OF THESE MANAGEMENT QUALITIES IMPORTANT FOR SUCCESS 1 TO 8 (MOST IMPORTANT FIRST)

☐ **Acting with Flexibility** — being able to behave in seemingly opposite ways such as being tough and at the same time compassionate, leading and letting others lead.

☐ **Balancing Personal and Work Life** — balancing work priorities with personal life so that neither is neglected.

☐ **Being a Quick Study** — quickly mastering new knowledge and skills

☐ **Building and Mending Relationships** — getting the cooperation of peers and clients, negotiate well, not alienating others.

☐ **Compassion and Sensitivity** — caring about the hopes and dreams of others, being sensitive to the needs of others.

☐ **Confronting Problem Subordinates** — moving quickly to remedy performance problems.

☐ **Decisiveness** — displaying a bias for action and calculated risks.

☐ **Doing Whatever it Takes** — persevering through adversity, taking full responsibility, seizing opportunities.

☐ **Hiring Talented People** — recruiting the best.

☐ **Integrity** — not blaming or abusing others, relying on substance and straightforwardness.

☐ **Leading Subordinates** — motivating subordinates, delegating to them, setting clear performance expectations.

☐ **Putting People at Ease** — having personal warmth and a good sense of humor.

☐ **Resourcefulness** — being a flexible problem solver, handling pressure and ambiguity, being a strategic thinker.

☐ **Self-awareness** — recognizing strengths and weaknesses, seeking corrective feedback.

☐ **Setting a Developmental Climate** — encouraging growth, leading by example, providing challenge and opportunity.

**Source:** Cynthia D. McCauley and Martha W. Hughes, "Human Service Administrators: Leadership Challenges and Competencies," *Proceedings*, Center for Creative Leadership, Independent Sector Spring Research Forum, 1991.

ence), resourcefulness (one point difference), leading subordinates (five point difference), setting a developmental climate (one point difference), and hiring talented staff (two point difference). It's not surprising that the nonprofit managers tended to value integrity, balancing personal and work life, compassion and sensitivity, and putting people at ease more highly than the business managers or that the corporate managers clearly valued decisiveness more than nonprofit managers did.

These findings are good news for businesspeople who wish to leave the private sector for the nonprofit world. If you exhibit most of the management qualities most highly valued in the corporate world, you possess most of the management characteristics also highly valued in the nonprofit sector.

In the three case studies that follow, think about the three abilities ranked the highest as they relate to managing charitable organizations. Flexibility is a critical skill that enables you to reconcile diverse demands on your time, your actions and your judgment. Decisions regarding organizational direction, program development, service delivery, and evaluating effectiveness are not easily reached because choices are rarely clear cut. The

### Ranking of Important Qualities for Managerial Success Found by McCauley and Hughes

| Management Quality | Managers at Nonprofits | | Corporate Managers | |
|---|---|---|---|---|
| | Rank | Percent Selecting | Rank | Percent Selecting |
| Acting with flexibility | 1 | 84% | 1 | 81% |
| Resourcefulness | 2 | 80% | 2 | 81% |
| Leading subordinates | 3 | 74% | 3 | 79% |
| Integrity | 4 | 70% | 9 | 57% |
| Setting a developmental climate | 5 | 64% | 5 | 63% |
| Hiring talent | 6 | 59% | 6 | 61% |
| Team orientation | 7 | 58% | 4 | 66% |
| Building and mending relationships | 8 | 48% | 10 | 52% |
| Doing whatever it takes | 9 | 47% | 8 | 57% |
| Balancing personal and work life | 10 | 42% | 13 | 24% |
| Compassion and sensitivity | 11 | 40% | 14 | 20% |
| Self–awareness | 12 | 34% | 12 | 25% |
| Putting people at ease | 13 | 34% | 15 | 19% |
| Decisiveness | 14 | 33% | 7 | 59% |
| Being a quick study | 15 | 22% | 11 | 34% |

presence of multiple objectives and priorities, diverse constituency groups, and the concerns of interdisciplinary staff requires an openness to the ideas of others and an ability to maintain balance within the organization.

# CASE STUDY IN FLEXIBILITY

Allen is the chief executive officer of a national voluntary health organization that raises over $40 million a year for medical research. He has a great responsibility to manage with flexibility. Its 200+ local chapters across the country raise money locally and some regionally. Each chapter must meet minimal performance standards. The organization is governed by an elite, national medical board that determines how the funds raised are to be used for research. Unions represent various employee groups. Allen's organization must coordinate its efforts with other national voluntary health agencies that also raise money for similar medical research purposes. And there are governmental agencies that constantly monitor their activities. Competing interests and conflicting agendas are constantly present. Allen balances the demands of these multiple constituencies very well because he possesses outstanding flexibility. Where did Allen work before? He was the head of public affairs for a major financial institution.

# CASE STUDY IN RESOURCEFULNESS

Resourcefulness is the ability to apply creativity to problem solving. The great majority of nonprofit organizations employ fewer that 50 people. A lack of financial, physical plant, and personnel resources are a fact of life for them. Managers who can imaginatively use scarce resources are highly valued in the nonprofit world.

Joan is the founding executive director of an early childhood development center in a marginal inner city neighborhood. She negotiated the original lease with a local church to use 1,700 square feet of space of its Sunday School rooms (vacant six days a week) for $50 a month. She persuaded a board member married to a hardware dealer to donate paint, lumber, and supplies. She staffed the center with three graduate students from a local university as unpaid interns for 30 hours each week. The parent advisory council she formed raised money to purchase educational materials and equipment. She was able to accomplish all of this because she has outstanding resourcefulness. What was her previous job? Joan was an investor relations coordinator for a small company.

# CASE STUDY IN LEADERSHIP

Leading subordinates requires a combination of skills that relate people to their jobs and their jobs to the big picture, the organization's mission. It starts with selecting the right staff, which requires an ability to judge people not solely on their ability to do the job but also on how they fit with others in the organization. Because no one is good at everything, we must remember to hire people on the basis of their strengths and not on the absence of weaknesses. Leading staff requires the ability to engender an integrated work effort, often called teamwork, where each staff member has a greater feeling of group ownership, a greater stake in the purpose of the organization, and still accepts individual responsibility for her particular job. Leading staff requires an ability to motivate and to keep staff focused, enthusiastic, cooperative, and productive often under very difficult circumstances.

Bob is the clinic manager for an association that opposes cruelty to animals. As is true in most metropolitan clinics, many more stray and abandoned cats and dogs are euthanized at Bob's clinic than are adopted. After a five–day holding period, dogs and cats not adopted are humanely destroyed by lethal injection. Bob has a dozen employees who help the veterinarians destroy as many as a dozen animals a day, six days a week, 12 months a year. Staff turnover is understandably high. To reduce turnover, Bob started scheduling periodic staff meetings where each employee has a turn at leading the group. They talk about their frustrations, stress, and anguish associated with the job. Every three months Bob rotates staff between the clinic and the shelter where animal adoption takes place. Bob has learned the interviewing techniques needed to select the right job applicants from the animal lovers who apply. Some candidates are too sensitive; others too callused. Bob has to find the happy medium.

Leading his staff is the toughest part of Bob's job. His ability to get his staff members to relate their work to the charitable mission of the organization is an important key to his success. He is successful because he is very skilled at leading subordinates. Bob's previous job? Bob used to sell advertising for a major magazine publisher.

# Classifying Your Nonprofit Interest

For job seekers, the nonprofit sector's diversity is both its most attractive attribute as well as its most confusing characteristic. You can find a nonprofit or charitable organization that addresses nearly every conceivable human need. But this does not mean that finding a job in the nonprofit industry is an easy task.

There may be only about a half dozen or so specific nonprofits among the plethora of nonprofit groups that will interest you enough and/or utilize your skills to make it worthwhile to even consider a career transition to the nonprofit sector. Many different factors will help you determine which organizations would make desirable employers for you, including the organization's mission and purpose, service delivery goals, budget size, and location. A cause that is really dear to your heart, such as for or against abortion rights, could be very controversial or risky to work for. You may feel more comfortable working for a small enterprise or you may find a large, complex environment more rewarding. You may thrive in an urban setting or, alternatively abhor the city life and prefer to work in a less congested area. You may be interested in working for an established institution or be motivated by the risk and struggle required to build and maintain a new or emerging charitable enterprise.

You can narrow your job search by taking these factors into consideration, as you would for any job. This focusing process is an essential step for ultimately targeting specific charities at which you wish to pursue employment opportunities.

But, how do you get to this point if you are not familiar with the full range of nonprofit organizations that exist? How can you assure that you have considered the full scope of the nonprofit industry to make certain that you have not overlooked potentially great employment opportunities? If you are completely open to consider working for almost any nonprofit, where do you start?

First you need to divide the nonprofit arena into its different fields. At even the broadest level of differentiation you can begin to form some assumptions about specific nonprofit settings that could interest you. The Internal Revenue Service has established a classification system for tax–exempt organizations that serves as a good place to start.

Section 501(c) of the Internal Revenue Code defines the conditions under which purposes and activities of a charitable entity must operate to be exempted from paying certain taxes, primarily federal income tax. Most of the nation's nonprofit entities — religious, educational, scientific, literary, and other similar organizations — fall within the 501(c)(3) subclassification. The other sub-classes under Section 501(c) identify the types of nonprofits more narrowly. The chart that follows shows the 20 501(c) classifications the IRS has established.

| IRS Classification | Description of Nonprofit Organizations |
|---|---|
| 501(c)(1) | Corporations organized by an act of Congress |
| 501(c)(2) | Title–holding corporations for exempt organizations |
| 501(c)(3) | Organizations whose nature is religious, educational, charitable, scientific, literary, test for public safety, foster certain national or international amateur sports competition, or prevent cruelty to children or animals |
| 501(c)(4) | Civic leagues, social welfare organizations, and local associations of employees |
| 501(c)(5) | Labor, agricultural and horticultural organizations |
| 501(c)(6) | Associations, business leagues, chambers of commerce, real estate boards |
| 501(c)(7) | Social and recreational clubs |
| 501(c)(8) | Fraternal beneficiary societies and associations |
| 501(c)(9) | Voluntary employees' beneficiary associations |
| 501(c)(10) | Domestic fraternal societies and associations |
| 501(c)(11) | Teachers' retirement fund associations |
| 501(c)(12) | Cemetery companies |

| IRS Classification | Description of Nonprofit Organizations |
|---|---|
| 501(c)(13) | Benevolent life-insurance associations, mutual ditch or irrigation companies, mutual cooperative telephone companies, etc. |
| 501(c)(14) | State-chartered credit unions and mutual reserve funds |
| 501(c)(15) | Mutual insurance companies or associations |
| 501(c)(16) | Cooperative organizations to finance crop operation |
| 501(c)(17) | Supplemental unemployment benefit trusts |
| 501(c)(18) | Employee funded pension trusts created before 1959 |
| 501(c)(19) | Post or organization of war veterans |
| 501(c)(20) | Group legal services plan organizations |

The Internal Revenue Service's division of nonprofit entities into different types of tax–exempt status is obviously quite broad. The table that starts on the next page offers a more in–depth list of the different charitable purposes and causes nonprofits serve. This list is not all–inclusive.

This table gives you an opportunity to see the incredibly broad scope of activities the nonprofit sector offers. Once you have perused it, it will be time to learn how to guide your career and job shift into the nonprofit world.

# CHARITABLE PURPOSES AND CAUSES

## ADVOCACY

- Birth control methods
- Capital punishment
- Ecology or conservation
- Firearms control
- Legalized abortion
- Medical care system
- National care system
- Population control
- Protection of consumer interests
- Racial integration
- Right to work
- Rights of criminal defendants
- Separation of church & state
- Stricter law enforcement
- Taxes or tax exemption
- U.S. foreign policy
- Urban renewal
- Use of intoxicating beverage
- Use of tobacco
- Welfare system

## BUSINESS AND PROFESSIONAL ORGANIZATIONS

- Business or professional group
- Chamber of Commerce
- Convention displays
- Industry trade shows
- Professional association
- Professional athletic league
- Real estate association
- Regulating business
- Research, developing & testing
- Tourist bureau

## CIVIL RIGHTS ACTIVITIES

- Defense of human or civil rights
- Elimination of prejudice and discrimination (race, religion, sex, national origin, disability, etc.)

## CONSERVATION, ENVIRONMENTAL, AND BEAUTIFICATION ACTIVITIES

- Combating or preventing pollution (air, water, etc.)
- Conservation, environmental, or beautification activities
- Garden club
- Preservation of natural resources (conservation)

- Preservation of scenic beauty
- Soil or water conservation
- Wildlife sanctuary or refuge

## CULTURAL, HISTORICAL, OR OTHER EDUCATIONAL ACTIVITIES

- Art exhibits
- Commemorative event (centennial, festival, pageant, etc.)
- Community theater
- Cultural exchanges with foreign country
- Cultural or historical activities
- Cultural performances
- Historical site, records, or reenactment
- Library and library activities
- Monument
- Museums, zoos
- Planetariums, etc.

## EMPLOYEE OR MEMBERSHIP BENEFIT ORGANIZATIONS

- Association of employees
- Fraternal beneficiary society, order, or association
- Pension or recruitment benefits
- Sick, accident, death, or similar benefits

## FARMING AND RELATED ACTIVITIES

- Agricultural group
- Breeders association
- Dairy heard improvement association
- Farm bureau
- Farmers' cooperative marketing or purchasing
- Financing crop operations
- Horticultural group

## HEALTH SERVICES AND RELATED ACTIVITIES

- Aid to people with disabilities
- Blood bank
- Care and housing for the aged
- Community health planning
- Cooperative hospital association organization
- Group medical practice association
- Health clinic
- Hospital
- Mental health care
- Nurse's register or bureau
- Nursing or convalescent home
- Prepaid group health plan
- Rescue and emergency service
- Rural medical facility

♦ Scientific research

## HOUSING ACTIVITIES

♦ Community residences for people with disabilities
♦ Fair housing
♦ Low– and moderate–income housing
♦ Poverty–level housing
♦ Housing for the agency
♦ Instruction & guidance on housing

## INDIVIDUALS AND MISCELLANEOUS ACTIVITIES

♦ Credit counseling and assistance
♦ Day care center
♦ Draft counseling
♦ Family planning
♦ Job training, counseling or assistance
♦ Marriage counseling
♦ Referral service (social agencies)
♦ Rehabilitating alcoholics, drug abusers, compulsive gamblers
♦ Rehabilitating convicts or ex–convicts
♦ Services for elderly people
♦ Supplying money, goods, or services to people who are poor

## INNER CITY OR COMMUNITY ACTIVITIES

♦ Area development, redevelopment, or renewal
♦ Attracting new industry or retaining
♦ Industry in an area
♦ Combating community deterioration
♦ Community promotion
♦ Community service organization
♦ Crime prevention
♦ Homeowners association
♦ Inner city or community benefit activities
♦ Loans or grants for minority businesses
♦ Voluntary fireman's organization or auxiliary

## LEGISLATIVE AND POLITICAL ACTIVITIES

♦ Legislative and political activities
♦ Propose, support, or oppose legislation
♦ Provide facilities or services for political campaign activities
♦ Support, oppose or rate political candidates
♦ Voter education

## LITIGATION AND LEGAL ASSISTANCE ACTIVITIES

- Legal aid to indigents
- Litigation or support of litigation
- Public interest litigation activities

## MISCELLANEOUS PURPOSES AND ACTIVITIES

- Achievement prizes & awards
- Advertising
- Cemetery or burial activities
- Community trust or component
- Consumer interest group
- Domestic organization with activities outside the U.S.
- Emergency or disaster aid fund
- Endowment fund or political services
- Erection or maintenance of public building or works
- Loans or credit reporting
- Native Americans (tribes, cultures, etc.)
- Patriotic activities
- Perpetual care fund
- Prevention of cruelty to animals
- Testing products for public safety
- Thrift shop, retail outlet, etc.
- Title holding corporation

## MUTUAL ORGANIZATIONS

- Corporation organized under an act of Congress
- Credit union
- Mutual ditch, irrigation, telephone
- Electric company or like organization
- Mutual insurance company
- Reserve funds or insurance for domestic cooperative bank, or mutual savings bank

## ORGANIZATIONS, MISCELLANEOUS ACTIVITIES

- Booster club
- Community Chest, United Fund
- Gifts, grants or loans to other organizations
- Non-financial services or facilities to other organizations

## RELIGIOUS ACTIVITIES

- Association or convention of churches
- Church auxiliary
- Church, synagogue
- Evangelism
- Missionary activities
- Religious order
- Religious publishing activities

## SCHOOLS, COLLEGES, AND RELATED ACTIVITIES

- Alumni association or group
- College athletic association
- Faculty group
- Fraternity or sorority
- Nursery school
- Parent to parent–teachers association
- Private school
- Scholarships for children of employees
- Special school for people with disabilities
- Student aid
- Student exchange with other country
- Student housing activities
- Student loans
- Student operated business

## SCIENTIFIC RESEARCH ACTIVITIES

- Contract or sponsored scientific research for industry
- Scientific research for government

## SPORTS, ATHLETIC, RECREATIONAL, AND SOCIAL ACTIVITIES

- Amateur athletic association
- Community center
- Community recreational facilities, (park,
- Playground, etc.)
- Country club
- Dinner club
- Dog club
- Fund raising athletic or sports event
- Hobby club
- Hunting or fishing club
- Swimming or tennis club
- Training in sports
- Travel tours
- Travel tours
- Variety club
- Women's club

## YOUTH ACTIVITIES

- Boy Scouts
- Boys Club, Little League, etc.
- Camp
- Care and housing of children (orphanage, etc.)
- Combat juvenile delinquency
- FFA, FHA, 4–H Club, etc.
- JCC, YMCA, YWCA, etc.
- Key club
- Prevention of cruelty to children

Source: *National Directory of Nonprofit Organizations* (Taft, 1990)

# WHAT INTERESTS YOU?

One criterion should initially guide your pursuit of nonprofit employment: an organization's appeal to you. Consider each nonprofit only in terms of its mission or purpose. Does it "grab you?" Does passion well up inside you just thinking about it? Forget about whether your current job title might fit within a nonprofit entity you are considering. Forget about making assumptions that you may not be qualified to work for that particular organization. Forget about everything except how much the organization appeals to you. "Appeal" can be defined on the basis of your responses to these three questions:

**1**    Do I passionately believe in the purpose of this organization?

**2**    Will I be energized going to work in this setting *every* day?

**3**    Will I be stimulated, intellectually and emotionally, by the kind of people who work at this organization?

Your responses to these three questions form the basis for what I call "Basic Appeal Criteria." The career transition to the nonprofit world is difficult enough without starting in an organization that only mildly motivates you. These Basic Appeal Criteria serve as a useful screening method to identify your particular interests. But they are only the start of the process for determining the nonprofit entities that will be the best fit for you.

# NONPROFIT PREFERENCE INDEXING

The Nonprofit Preference Index (NPPI)© offers a starting point for beginning to put many of these preference factors into perspective. I developed this self–administered preference survey to help people making the transition into the nonprofit sector explore and classify their own nonprofit interests. By evaluating and indexing your responses to the NPPI survey, it is possible to identify one or more organizational profiles that you can use to target potential employers in the nonprofit world.

The NPPI consists of a list of brief profiles of 56 actual nonprofit organizations. Step One of the NPPI asks you to rate each organization profile from one to four using these ranking criteria:

**1** = Unappealing to you
**2** = Moderately unappealing to you
**3** = Moderately appealing to you
**4** = Highly appealing to you

### IF YOU DON'T OWN ...

If you have borrowed this book from a library or career center and do *not* own it, please photocopy pages 48 through 57 and complete the NPPI steps on your photocopy. Please do *not* write in this book. On behalf of your library or career center, thank you.

Step Two involves entering your ratings on the NPPI Score Sheet that follows the organizational profiles. Step Three requires you to do some addition and Step Four involves some self–analysis of your results.

Before you start the survey, a word of caution is warranted. You probably will be sympathetic to the

mission and purpose of many of the organizational profiles described in this survey. Rating a particular organization as "unappealing" does *not* make you heartless nor
does it mean that you necessarily disagree with its purpose. All it means is that the organization does not *appeal* to *your* interests. Remember that the purpose of
this exercise is to determine how appealing the organization is to *your own interests*. It is *not* an assessment of
your sympathies for any organization or what it does.

# NONPROFIT PREFERENCE INDEX

## Basic Appeal Criteria

☑ Do I passionately believe in the purpose of this
organization?

☑ Will I be energized going to work in this setting
*every* day?

☑ Will I be stimulated, intellectually and emotionally,
by the kind of people who work at this
organization?

---

### PREFERENCE RATINGS

**1** = Unappealing to you

**2** = Moderately unappealing to you

**3** = Moderately appealing to you

**4** = Highly appealing to you

# STEP 1: RATING PROFILES

## Nonprofit Organization Profiles

### Rate each profile from 1 (unappealing) to 4 highly appealing)

1 [1] A 90–bed community hospital that serves a multi–county rural area.

2 [4] A four–year coed liberal arts college with 4,500 students located in a metropolitan city.

3 [4] A large museum of contemporary art in a major city.

4 [2] A family service agency with a $1 million budget that provides counseling, emergency shelter and child care programs in a metropolitan city.

5 [ ] A private, nonprofit nature center and wildlife preserve.

6 [ ] A professional membership organization comprised of plastic and reconstructive surgeons.

7 [ ] An auto safety institute with a $3 million budget located in a major city that provides an independent source of information for the general public.

8 [3] A national advocacy organization that supports legislation and carries out programs for literacy training in America.

9 [1] A professional membership organization of business and financial officers of colleges and universities across the country.

10 [2] A large zoological park that serves a major urban/suburban area.

11 [2] A national disaster relief organization that organizes and deploys volunteers to all areas of the country when needed.

**12** `3` A $10 million youth development agency that provides recreational, tutoring, remedial education, and job training programs for inner city youth.

**13** `2` An established, nonprofit theater group with a $750,000 budget serving a metropolitan audience.

**14** `2` An independent college prep school for 1,100 boys and girls located in an upscale suburban area.

**15** `1` A national voluntary organization with dozens of local offices around the country that raises money for juvenile diabetes research.

**16** `1` A nursing home in a large retirement village complex serving a metropolitan city.

**17** `1` An early childhood development center serving a three-county rural population.

**18** `3` A science and natural history museum with a $3 million budget located in a metropolitan area.

**19** `2` A national ballet company that performs internationally.

**20** `1` A religiously–affiliated, 25–bed residential center for emotionally and behaviorally disturbed adolescents located in a secluded area.

**21** `2` A metropolitan–based nonprofit organization that promotes and organizes recycling and waste management programs for neighborhood organizations.

**22** `1` A professional membership organization comprised of teachers at private, nonprofit independent college preparatory schools.

**23** `1` A small Native American rights organization located near a major American Indian reservation community.

**24** `1` A membership organization that provides training and development for alcohol and drug abuse counselors.

25 ☐ A national organization that operates programs for the preservation and propagation of endangered plants and animals.

26 ☐ A local network of senior citizen day care centers and home–delivered meal programs for shut–ins in a metropolitan city.

27 ☐ An historic preservation society that owns and operates a small museum in a rural county.

28 ☐ A major private university in the middle of an urban setting.

29 ☐ A noted blood research center located in a major city and affiliated with a university medical school .

30 ☐ A national organization that engages in educational policy research, program evaluation, and achievement testing that directs learning demonstration projects.

31 ☐ A large performing arts center with six affiliate arts organizations that deliver programs mostly to audiences in small cities within a 100–mile radius.

32 ☐ A major food bank operation that collects donated food to distribute to dozens of city and suburban social service agencies that run feeding programs for the homeless.

33 ☐ A prominent farm land and soil conservation organization that operates in a mostly rural area.

34 ☐ A professional membership organization that advocates preserving natural wetlands for waterfowl in North America.

35 ☐ A major minority rights organization located in a major city.

**36** 〔1〕 An association whose membership consists of juvenile court judges.

**37** 〔1〕 A small independent research laboratory in a major city that provides planning, development, and evaluation of waste management programs in the region.

**38** 〔2〕 A two–year community college with 3,500 adults and traditional students serving a three–county metropolitan area.

**39** 〔1〕 A hospice program located in a remote area for terminal cancer patients and people with AIDS .

**40** 〔1〕 A religiously–affiliated coed college with 400 students located in a small town.

**41** 〔2〕 A national organization that provides funding and support for the visual arts.

**42** 〔1〕 An arboretum, botanical research and horticultural garden located in a predominantly rural area with an operating budget of $600,000.

**43** 〔3〕 A small think–tank organization in a metropolitan community that researches global economic policy and practice.

**44** 〔1〕 A professional association of attorneys, social workers, urban planners, and others who advocate and develop programs for open and fair housing.

**45** 〔1〕 A national advocacy organization that supports legislation and develops programs to assist people with physical disabilities.

**46** 〔1〕 A nonprofit credit union that furnishes low–interest loans to the working poor in a rural area.

**47** 〔1〕 A regional symphony orchestra that performs mostly audiences in small cities on a $2 million budget.

**48** `1` A national teacher training center that provides continuing teacher education at over 60 sites across the country.

**49** `2` An advocacy organization in a metropolitan city that studies and supports community efforts in urban renewal and development.

**50** `1` A national organization with dozens of affiliates that provide rehabilitation and job retraining programs for adults with work–related disabilities.

**51** `2` A national organization that provides audio recordings of books, magazines, textbooks, and newspapers for people who are blind.

**52** `1` A major five–hospital nonprofit healthcare system with comprehensive programs that serves a sprawling urban/suburban area .

**53** `1` A national research institute concerned with the development of alternative sources of energy.

**54** `2` A professional association of children's museum exhibit designers and fabricators.

**55** `2` A religiously–affiliated health and dental care clinic with a budget of $1.5 million that serves patients at an inner city location.

**56** `1` A small, but venerable organization that advocates for health care access and distribution to serve the poor in rural areas.

## STEP 2: CHARTING YOUR RATINGS

Enter the rating you assigned to each of the 56 profiles on the previous pages in the chart that follows.

Print your rating for each numbered profile in the appropriate blank box in the numbered row for that profile.

| Profile Number | Organizational Classification | | | | | | | Location | | | Size | | | |
|---|---|---|---|---|---|---|---|---|---|---|---|---|---|---|
| | Health Care | Education | Cultural | Human Services | Conservation | Association | Public Interest | Urban/Suburban | Metropolitan | Rural | National/International | Large/Complex | Average/Medium | Small |
| 1 | | | | | | | | | | | | | | |
| 2 | | | | | | | | | | | | | | |
| 3 | | | | | | | | | | | | | | |
| 4 | | | | | | | | | | | | | | |
| 5 | | | | | | | | | | | | | | |
| 6 | | | | | | | | | | | | | | |
| 7 | | | | | | | | | | | | | | |
| 8 | | | | | | | | | | | | | | |
| 9 | | | | | | | | | | | | | | |
| 10 | | | | | | | | | | | | | | |
| 11 | | | | | | | | | | | | | | |
| 12 | | | | | | | | | | | | | | |
| 13 | | | | | | | | | | | | | | |
| 14 | | | | | | | | | | | | | | |

| Profile Number | Organizational Classification | | | | | | | Location | | | Size | | | |
| --- | --- | --- | --- | --- | --- | --- | --- | --- | --- | --- | --- | --- | --- | --- |
| | Health Care | Education | Cultural | Human Services | Conservation | Association | Public Interest | Urban/Suburban | Metropolitan | Rural | National/International | Large/Complex | Average/Medium | Small |
| 15 | X | | | | | | | | | | X | | | |
| 16 | X | | | | | | | | X | | | | X | |
| 17 | | X | | | | | | | | X | | | | |
| 18 | | | X | | | | | | | X | | | | |
| 19 | | | X | | | | | | | | X | | | |
| 20 | | | X | | | | | | X | | | | | X |
| 21 | | | | X | | | | | X | | | X | | |
| 22 | | | | | X | | | X | | | | | X | |
| 23 | | | | | | X | | | | X | | X | | |
| 24 | | | | X | | | | | X | | | | | |
| 25 | | | | X | | | | | | X | | | X | |
| 26 | | | | | | | | | X | | | | | |
| 27 | | | X | | | | | | | X | | | | X |
| 28 | | X | | | | | | X | | | | | | |
| 29 | X | | | | | | | | | | X | | | |

| Profile Number | Organizational Classification | | | | | | | Location | | | Size | | | |
|:---:|:---:|:---:|:---:|:---:|:---:|:---:|:---:|:---:|:---:|:---:|:---:|:---:|:---:|:---:|
| | Health Care | Education | Cultural | Human Services | Conservation | Association | Public Interest | Urban/Suburban | Metropolitan | Rural | National/International | Large/Complex | Average/Medium | Small |
| 30 | | ☐ | | | | | | | | ☐ | ☐ | | | |
| 31 | | | ☐ | | | | | | ☐ | | | | ☐ | |
| 32 | | | | ☐ | | | | ☐ | | | | ☐ | | |
| 33 | | | | | ☐ | | | | | ☐ | | | ☐ | |
| 34 | | | | | | ☐ | | | | ☐ | | ☐ | | |
| 35 | | | | | | | ☐ | ☐ | | | | ☐ | | |
| 36 | | | | | ☐ | | | | | ☐ | | | | ☐ |
| 37 | | | | ☐ | | | | ☐ | | | | | ☐ | |
| 38 | | ☐ | | | | | | | | ☐ | | | | ☐ |
| 39 | ☐ | | | | | | | ☐ | | | | ☐ | | |
| 40 | | ☐ | | | | | | | | ☐ | | | ☐ | |
| 41 | | | ☐ | | | | | | ☐ | | | | | ☐ |
| 42 | | | | ☐ | | | | | | ☐ | | | | ☐ |
| 43 | | | | | | ☐ | | | ☐ | | | | | |
| 44 | | | | | | | ☐ | | | | | | | ☐ |

| Profile Number | Organizational Classification | | | | | | | Location | | | Size | | | |
|---|---|---|---|---|---|---|---|---|---|---|---|---|---|---|
| | Health Care | Education | Cultural | Human Services | Conservation | Association | Public Interest | Urban/Suburban | Metropolitan | Rural | National/International | Large/Complex | Average/Medium | Small |
| 45 | | | | | | | X | | | | X | | | |
| 46 | | | | X | | | | | | | | | | X |
| 47 | | | X | | | | | | | X | | | | |
| 48 | | X | | | | | | | | X | | | | |
| 49 | | | | | | | X | | X | | | | | |
| 50 | X | | | | | | | | | | | X | | |
| 51 | | | | X | | | | | | | | X | | |
| 52 | X | | | | | | | X | | | | | X | |
| 53 | | | | | X | | | | | | X | | | |
| 54 | | | | | | X | | | | | | | X | |
| 55 | X | | | | | | | | X | | | | X | |
| 56 | | | | | | | | X | | X | | | | X |
| Column Total | | | | | | | | | | | | | | |

# STEP 3: CALCULATIONS

Add the numbers in each column of the above table to get the "Column Total" for each of the 14 columns. Take these "Column Totals" and print them in the "Column Totals" column in the table below labeled "Step 3: Your Calculations. Next, perform the simple division as shown in the center column to get the "Average Index Score" for each nonprofit classification, location choice, and size

## STEP 3: YOUR CALCULATIONS

| Preference Category | Column Totals | Divide by | Average Index Score | Total Number of "4" Ratings |
|---|---|---|---|---|
| Health Care | _____ | ÷ 8 = | _____ | _____ |
| Education | _____ | ÷ 8 = | _____ | _____ |
| Cultural | _____ | ÷ 8 = | _____ | _____ |
| Human Services | _____ | ÷ 8 = | _____ | _____ |
| Conservation | _____ | ÷ 8 = | _____ | _____ |
| Association | _____ | ÷ 8 = | _____ | _____ |
| Public Interest | _____ | ÷ 8 = | _____ | _____ |
| Urban/Suburban | _____ | ÷ 12 = | _____ | _____ |
| Metropolitan | _____ | ÷ 12 = | _____ | _____ |
| Rural | _____ | ÷ 12 = | _____ | _____ |
| National/ International | _____ | ÷ 14 = | _____ | _____ |
| Large/Complex | _____ | ÷ 14 = | _____ | _____ |
| Average/Medium | _____ | ÷ 14 = | _____ | _____ |
| Small | _____ | ÷ 14 = | _____ | _____ |

option. Finally, put the number of "4" ratings you gave each classification in the last column.

# STEP 4: INTERPRETING YOUR RESULTS

The NPPI identifies the consistency in your responses so it can help focus your job search. Nearly all of the 56 organizational profiles include information on all three preference factors. As you will soon see, your scoring can indicate the extent to which an organization's size, location, and geographic scope — in addition to its focus — influence how it appeals to you. Understanding how these factors combine to lead to your preferences is critical to successfully focusing your nonprofit job search.

Interpreting your NPPI scores is an art, not a science, especially when your "average index scores" are very close for two or more choices within a preference category. Probably the best way to explain how to interpret your own NPPI scores — especially if they are close— is to use the real life example of Ellen, a 32–year old financial services manager for a branch bank. After completing the NPPI survey, she added the columns, did the math, and came up with the scores that appear on page 59.

Of the seven organizational classifications (Health Care, Education, etc.), Ellen's greatest interest appeared to be in cultural and human service organizations where her average index scores were both 3.125. Awarding five of her seven "4" rankings to cultural and human service organization profiles seems to confirm this interest.

It did not surprise Ellen that the cultural area interested her so much. As a young child, she took seven years of Suzuki violin lessons and played competitively in high school. Today, she holds season tickets to the local symphony orchestra.

But she was surprised that she had ranked human service organizations just as highly. She had never felt any particular leaning in that direction. But when she looked again at the human service organization profiles in the NPPI, she found that the ones she ranked the highest were in children and youth services. With that insight, things began to fall into place for her. Years ago

## EXAMPLE: ELLEN'S NPPI CALCULATIONS

| Preference Category | Column Totals | Divide by | Average Index Score | Total Number of "4" Ratings |
|---|---|---|---|---|
| Health Care | 19 | ÷ 8 = | 2.375 | 2 |
| Education | 19 | ÷ 8 = | 2.375 | 0 |
| Cultural | 25 | ÷ 8 = | 3.125 | 3 |
| Human Services | 25 | ÷ 8 = | 3.125 | 2 |
| Conservation | 15 | ÷ 8 = | 1.875 | 0 |
| Association | 11 | ÷ 8 = | 1.375 | 0 |
| Public Interest | 18 | ÷ 8 = | 2.250 | 0 |
| Urban/Suburban | 32 | ÷ 12 = | 2.67 | 2 |
| Metropolitan | 34 | ÷ 12 = | 2.83 | 5 |
| Rural | 30 | ÷ 12 = | 2.50 | 0 |
| National/International | 27 | ÷ 14 = | 1.929 | 1 |
| Large/Complex | 37 | ÷ 14 = | 2.643 | 3 |
| Average/Medium | 34 | ÷ 14 = | 2.429 | 4 |
| Small | 33 | ÷ 14 = | 2.357 | 0 |

she had considered becoming a music teacher. Her high index scores in cultural and human service organizations led Ellen to think that she might be able to combine her interest in music with her interest in children and youth — potentially an ideal career track to follow.

Ellen then looked at her scores regarding location of the organization: urban/suburban, metropolitan, and rural. The "Metropolitan" category not only produced her highest "average index score," but it also garnered five of the seven "4" rankings that she handed out. Not surprisingly, Ellen currently lives in a large urban area and enjoys it. She was not really in a position to relocate for any new job. She thought that growing up in Indianapolis might have had something to do with her preference for metropolitan areas. She also noted that an urban/suburban setting was her second choice. She decided to focus her nonprofit search in metropolitan areas.

Like you, the third preference category Ellen had to evaluate was how large a nonprofit entity she wanted to work for. Her "average index score" of 2.643 for a large, complex organization was *only slightly higher* than the 2.429 "average index score" for an "average/medium" sized group. Her two top choices flip–flopped when she considered the number of "4" rankings she assigned to each: four to average/medium sized groups and only three "4" rankings to large, complex organizations. Since the scores were so close, she realized that she would probably enjoy working in either size nonprofit. This wasn't surprising since her current job at the branch bank — an average, medium–sized work site — is part of the much larger parent bank — a large, complex institution.

By completing the NPPI and carefully evaluating her results, Ellen discovered several important preference factors to guide her nonprofit job search. The preferences for a medium/average or large/complex cultural or human service organization located in an urban or metropolitan area led her to focus on three specific types of opportunities: an inner-city arts education program with a $6 million annual budget that serves highly talented but economically disadvantaged young people; a symphony orchestra, with a $30 million annual budget, that sponsors a well-known Young Performers competition; and a youth development agency, operating under a $3 million annual budget, that trains teenagers for careers in film and television production. Each of these opportunities fit within the interests she identified using the NPPI.

Use Ellen's approach to help you interpret your own NPPI results. Don't be surprised if you also arrive at close scores for several organizational profiles. It is also likely that you may have close results for organizational size and location as well. Remember, the NPPI helps you focus your nonprofit job search, not pinpoint it.

The chapters that follow will help you narrow the focus of your search for a nonprofit position. The NPPI simply helps you make sense out of the multitude of charitable organizations that exist so you can better focus your nonprofit career and job search in the areas that appeal to your own personal preferences.

# Strategic
# Volunteerism

*"One of the problems I seem to be having is my
lack of hands–on experience in a not–for–profit. I
get the feeling that the [nonprofit organization]
people I've talked to use this as a justification to
avoid hiring someone who wants to leave the for–
profit world for the not–for–profit."*
*— A frustrated business professional in transition*

Thanks to our American culture, the odds are over-
whelmingly strong that you already have connections
within the nonprofit community even though you have
always worked in the business world. Nowhere is philanthropy more widespread and so much a part of a nation's core values than in the United States. The financial support of private nonprofit organizations through
individual charitable contributions of cash and volun-

tary services is much more extensive than in any other major industrialized country including Japan, Great Britain, and Canada. The American Association of Fund Raising Executives reports that, in 1998, U.S. corporations, foundations, bequests, and individuals donated over $175 billion to nonprofits, about two percent of the gross domestic product. Tax–deductible charitable contributions from individuals account for 77 percent of all contributions to nonprofit organizations. These cash donations are supplemented by millions of hours of volunteer services every year.

The spirit of charitable giving in the U.S. is so widespread that it would be highly unusual to find a business professional who has never made a charitable donation or never served in a volunteer role for a nonprofit organization. One reason for this is that most of us were indoctrinated to philanthropy at an early age in conjunction with church, synagogue, or mosque activities. As a child I watched my father reach into his pocket every Sunday morning as the ushers passed the plate in church. Its rim was a rich polished walnut with ornate designs and a red velvet pouch neatly tacked to its underside. As the plate passed by my eyes, green currency sticking out, I began to associate church with charity. Of course I did not understand it in those terms. But unlike buying goods in a store, when my father gave the church money it was obvious to even my young eyes that he received nothing tangible in return.

The power of that simple act, in different ways and at different times, has been imbedded deeply in the American psyche. From the earliest time in this country, organized religious groups were the catalysts for philanthropy. They were the driving force behind the establishment of most of our nonprofit hospitals, private colleges, and human service agencies. Religion–affiliated organizations still account for the majority of hospital beds and private college classrooms in the United States. It is not surprising that the largest segment of the workforce in the fields of health care and private higher education is employed by institutions sponsored by or affiliated with an organized religion. Charitable giving to these organizations as well as to thousands of independent charities has become a social expectation and a personal responsibility, one most of us have accepted graciously.

With over 56 percent of American adults serving as volunteers according to a 1999 national survey by the Independent Sector, it's not surprising that most business professionals become involved in several charitable causes over the course of their careers, both as a donor and a volunteer. We are asked to serve on boards of directors, help with fund raising, participate as an advisor on specific policy and administrative councils where your business background may help, and in some cases provide direct services to reduce the organization's operating costs. A large social service agency, for example, may use volunteers to assist teachers with preschoolers in a Head Start program in a housing project. A group home for teenage girls with emotional troubles may utilize volunteers to tutor the young women in math and science. A children's hospital may uses volunteers as "rockers" for crack cocaine babies. A food bank may send volunteers to deliver home meals to shut–ins and senior citizens with disabilities. The list is endless, and so are the needs.

For most business professionals, volunteer activities are considered civic responsibilities, directed by their particular interest in a cause, the amount of time they have available to devote and sometimes by one's expertise or avocational abilities. There is a commitment involved in volunteering, a commitment to giving up the time you could be devoting to other personal interests; a commitment to an organization which may rely heavily on volunteers to reduce its expenses; a commitment to those who depend on the services the nonprofit provides.

For those business professionals who want to make a career transition to the nonprofit sector, however, volunteering takes on a whole new meaning. It becomes an important activity to help position you for employment in the nonprofit workplace. I refer to it as *Strategic Volunteerism*. Not only can it help you get hired in the nonprofit sector, but it can also further your assimilation into the nonprofit culture.

## STRATEGIC VOLUNTEERISM IN ACTION

It's only logical that the more experience and expertise you have at a particular job skill, the more likely it is that you will be looked upon with a higher degree of credibility — in both the business world and the nonprofit sector. Formal education notwithstanding, you learn by doing; on–the–job experience is essential to achieving success at work. When it comes to on–the–job experience, the nonprofit sector offers something the business world cannot: volunteer opportunities.

Volunteerism provides an opportunity to gain experience working in a charitable enterprise without being employed by a nonprofit organization — a pretty re-markable opportunity! If chosen to serve on a charity's board of directors, you get to learn the "business" inside and out while performing your fiduciary duties as a di-rector. You have an opportunity to develop long–range strategic plans, establish policies for program delivery, decide important budget and fiscal matters, shape mar-keting and development strategies, oversee personnel situations, and deal with regulatory and government is-sues. You learn the operations and the most effective ways to implement the organization's mission. In short, you gain experience "working" in a nonprofit without ac-tually being on the payroll.

Human service organizations, hospitals, cultural or-ganizations, and other charities provide a great variety of volunteer opportunities that can get you behind the scenes and provide a significant inside view. People who volunteer at this level are those with a high interest in the mission of the nonprofit organization. They would not put in the time if they were not committed to the cause. While that may go without saying, I point it out because when you are trying to position yourself to land a job in the nonprofit sector, the nature of the volunteer roles you have played, or the volunteer responsibilities you seek, have significant implications for the types of nonprofit employment opportunities you may pursue.

In the same way your record of business accomplish-ments and skills defines who you are to a prospective corporate employer, your record of voluntary affilia-tions, activities, and responsibilities can define who you are to a prospective employer in the nonprofit sector. Re-gardless of the nature of your business experiences, your volunteer responsibilities always can provide the common ground for conversation between you and a potential nonprofit employer. You immediately can share experiences that are familiar in charitable work and thereby establish your credibility in the nonprofit sector. You become "one of them" — assimilated! You are more likely to be accepted within the nonprofit community because you will have acquired some of its culture thanks to your experiences as a volunteer.

How do you decide which volunteer responsibilities will most effectively expedite your transition to a nonprofit career and job? With the hundreds of volunteer opportunities that exist, it is important to first understand that the nonprofit organization for which you decide to volunteer does not have to be the one for which you want to work. Obviously, you can wind up working for an organization at which you've been a volunteer; it happens frequently. Given the right set of circumstances and a lot of good timing and luck, this can be a serendipitous path to landing a great nonprofit job. But don't expect your first volunteer role to turn into a paid staff job. The reasons for this will become clearer as you understand more about the concept of Strategic Volunteerism.

To link your volunteer responsibilities to your job–search strategy, first return to your NPPI results in Chapter 3. Make nonprofit entities that fit the organizational profile you rated the highest your volunteering target. When identifying specific volunteer opportunities, it is important that you consider only those organizational settings that you rated the highest.

## THE KEY VOLUNTEER ROLE: BOARD OF DIRECTORS

Much has been written about volunteerism in the charitable sector. But one area of volunteerism has captured by far the most attention in the nonprofit world:

the volunteer board of directors. The law in every state requires that every corporation, whether profit–making or nonprofit, must have a board of directors or board of trustees. A board of directors exists to govern the charity, just as it governs a business or a city council governs a city. Just as a city council adopts a city charter or a state legislature adopts a state constitution, a nonprofit's board of directors adopt articles of incorporation and bylaws as its primary organizing instruments. And just as a town council is the highest and final local authority responsible to the public, the board of directors of a nonprofit entity is the highest and final authority responsible to the public on whose behalf it operates the charity that it governs.

Each organizational profile presented in the NPPI in Chapter 3, and each one you selected as highly preferable to pursue in your career transition, has a board of directors. This is the key volunteer responsibility in every nonprofit organization. This is the strategic volunteer role you should pursue if you wish to eventually secure a job in the nonprofit world.

Serving as a director on the governing board will give you access to information and people as well as hands–on experience in overseeing operation of the charity. It can provide you with important networking opportunities because it allows you to work among a group of people, paid staff and volunteers, who share similar values, contacts, and interests. Many of the functional skills you possess may be called upon immediately in response to the organization's need for certain types of business or professional backgrounds and experiences. Through the statutory fiduciary responsibility bestowed on board members, you assume a level of accountability consistent with your desire to support the charitable goals. There is clearly a strategic advantage in serving on a board of directors and there are many organizations that will welcome you if you indicate an interest in serving.

Conversely, it can be difficult to get elected to certain boards depending on the nature of the charitable organization. The great majority of directors serve on boards because they were recommended by a friend, a co-worker, or a business associate who serves or has served on the board. If you do not have these kinds of contacts, it will be more difficult to get elected to board service. In addition, certain boards are highly selective in their nominating process in order to maintain a specific or homogeneous profile. These boards may be more difficult to join as well. Alternative ways to affiliate with such organizations are discussed later in this chapter.

## Finding the Board That's Right for You

Although every board of directors operates at least a little bit differently, they can be categorized according to their governing styles. This is important because the Strategic Volunteering process requires that you understand these different governing styles so you end up on the board that is right for you.

So, what is the "right" board? It is the board that operates in such a manner that it provides you with a level of participation that enhances your career transition opportunities. Each board has a governing "style" of its own and its manner of operating will greatly affect the kind of strategic volunteer board experience you can expect.

Every board of directors operates under both formal and informal structures. The organization's bylaws dictate the board's formal structure and establishes the procedures for conducting board business. Most boards operate under the classic pyramidal structure of authority starting with a chairperson or president at the top, secretary, treasurer, other officers and committee chairpeople. You can pick a dozen sets of bylaws and they all tend to read much the same. The Internal Revenue Service even requires that the bylaws of tax–exempt charities include certain standard language for dissolution of the organization and the use of certain assets.

More important than the board's formal structure is its informal structure, which is usually more varied and more proactive. In her book, *Trusteeship in the Private College,* Miriam Mason Wood reports on this informal operating style in behavioral and relational terms. Wood explains that differences in actual board operating styles are reflected primarily in the relationships between board members and the chief executive officer, as well as between the CEO and the organization's different constituencies. The differences in these relationships are illustrated by the varying group norms that govern the sources and uses of information pertaining to the institution as well as information flow between the CEO and the board and between the CEO and the organization's constituencies. Wood identifies three major models of operating style. You should take into account the three different models of board behavior and relationships when strategically selecting the organization or organizations on whose boards you might wish to serve.

## THE RUBBER STAMP BOARD

The Ratifying or "Rubber Stamp" Board is most common where the chief executive officer is an exceptionally strong leader and manager, where she has occupied the CEO seat many years, and where board members represent an "old guard" composed of longtime directors. Essentially, the directors on these boards abdicate their responsibility to the CEO. They rely almost completely on the advice and direction of the chief executive. The board has virtually no interaction with other key administrative staff such as the finance officer or development officer. The board gets its information from one source: the CEO. It is the CEO's recommendation that is the most crucial information for the board in its decision making.

The Ratifying Board is considered rather old–fashioned under modern standards. The style of a Ratifying Board does little to foster volunteer participation. The old guard element serves to protect the chief executive, and the CEO uses the strengths of the individual board members, often underscored by wealth and social position, to preserve each member's status on the board. It is very difficult to assimilate into such a closed system. It does little to help you learn about the nonprofit's operations. Yet, this operating style is not necessarily "wrong" nor is it out of compliance with any regulatory requirements. The group norm is not one that provides for the kind of apprenticeship opportunities you should experience in your transition process.

## THE PARTICIPATORY BOARD

In contrast, the operating style of the Participatory Board is more likely to include board involvement in day–to–day management decisions. The Participatory Board's culture more closely resembles a family than an organization, with the chairperson as the head of the household. Lines of communication between board members and program staff, among community factions and the board, and in some cases among service recipients, are all open and seldom limited by the chief executive officer's role. Other senior staff members — not just the CEO — are likely to attend board meetings. This approach usually ensures that the board's focus will be on operating and program decisions. This type of board does not consider the CEO as a powerful figure and, in fact, the CEO is often a compliant personality type. Committees often work in a free-wheeling style and their reports to the full board often provoke long discussions that duplicate the committees' work.

The Participatory Board is a hands-on board that is exposed to the greatest amount of detailed information and a far higher level of involvement in operations than under any other board model. From an organizing standpoint, this operating style is probably the least efficient way to govern. The role of the CEO is diminished to the point of being nearly superfluous among other senior staff and the board sometimes wastes its time on short-term operating problems rather than policy-setting for the long term.

But this type of board does much more to facilitate your Strategic Volunteerism and assimilation into a nonprofit entity's "corporate" culture. If you find yourself on this board you may often get frustrated with the amount of resource duplication and stymied if you attempt to get the board to focus on long-term issues. But you will get an experience in nonprofit organization management and operations that can rival many paid staff positions.

## THE CORPORATE BOARD

Under the "Corporate Board" style of operating, a board seeks to govern the nonprofit organization as if it were a business. The majority of board members, and especially the chairperson, are usually experienced business executives. They are significantly involved in framing issues of finance, asset management, property acquisition, and capital improvement — namely the things that they typically focus on in their corporate positions. In this model the board requires a strong, but not autocratic, chief executive officer who assumes full management authority over the operations of the organization.

It is typical for the board, especially when it is a large one, to appoint an executive committee headed by the board's chairperson. The executive committee conducts frequent meetings with the CEO and digs deep into issues before consideration by the entire board. Under this arrangement, the chief executive controls the executive committee's agenda and pulls together and disseminates information he deems relevant to the executive committee. Issues of program or service delivery to the organization's constituents are of much less interest to the board members who believe this is the CEO's exclusive domain.

The Corporate Board operating style is usually the culture of a well–organized, homogeneous, efficient, high–energy group. The issues discussed tend to focus on mission, policy, and long–term strategy. The opinions of board members can be diverse and stimulating. Meetings are not a forum to nit–pick the CEO nor second guess her decisions.

This style of operating can be instructive during your career transition in large part due to a level of professionalism that ensures effective participation of all board members and a sense of purpose that is quite exact. However, there can be a danger for boards that focus nearly exclusively on the "business" of running a nonprofit while neglecting the program and service components that actually support its charitable purpose. Skewed too far in the business direction, this board style can sometimes detract from your Strategic Volunteerism and assimilation objectives. As a board member, you will find a need to balance your desire for more detailed information with the board's need to run the nonprofit entity like a business.

# RESEARCHING ORGANIZATIONAL BOARDS

In reality, these informal board operating styles tend to change over time to create a blend of styles as opposed to the exclusive models just described. A relatively new nonprofit organization's operating style may change with the introduction of new board members or with the election of a new chairperson or chief executive officer. Styles change as staffs and programs grow and as organizational information becomes more complex. Older, established organizations may not change their style for decades, particularly where the key board leadership and the CEO have remained the same for decades. Yet, whether an organization is new or old, established or emerging, does not always imply its board will follow a particular operating style. Strategic Volunteerism requires you to carefully assess on a case–by–case basis the different board volunteer opportunities to determine which may be the best for you.

How do you gather information on an organization's board of directors, and its formal and informal operating structures? This information is more readily available than you might imagine. Do not, however, assume there is any uniformity within a nonprofit field. You must tread  carefully when seeking what some people may deem to be "sensitive" information, even though most nonprofit operating information is considered public information.

Use the following primary and secondary sources to gather information on an organization's board of directors that will help you devise your approach to Strategic Volunteerism and help you identify the specific nonprofit organizations at which to volunteer.

## PRIMARY INFORMATION SOURCES

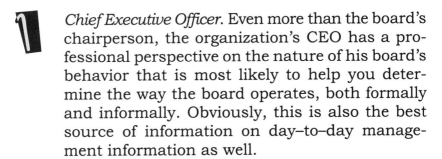

*Chief Executive Officer.* Even more than the board's chairperson, the organization's CEO has a professional perspective on the nature of his board's behavior that is most likely to help you determine the way the board operates, both formally and informally. Obviously, this is also the best source of information on day–to–day management information as well.

*Board Leadership.* Directors who are seen as true leaders on the board are often those who do not serve as officers. The absence of an office-holding title can give an informality to a director's discussion of board style that will provide you with important information.

*Past Organizational Officers.* A past chief executive officer or financial head of an organization, a former board chairman, key members of an executive committee, and former members of the senior management group — these are all valuable sources of information on both the current board and the board's history.

# SECONDARY INFORMATION SOURCES

 *Annual Reports.* Most nonprofits spend the time and money to produce a fairly detailed annual document that provides an audited financial statement, program achievements, service statistics, lists of donors, affiliations with constituent groups, and a listing of the members of the board of directors. You can almost always obtain a copy of an organization's annual report simply by asking. A helpful technique in your assessment process is to get a copy of annual reports for the past ten years or so to get a sense of turnover among board members.

 *Long Range or Strategic Plan.* In contrast to studying an organization's history by reviewing its annual reports, the charity's long range plan will give you at least two good pieces of information about the organization's future: the goals it is attempting to achieve over the next few years; and, if a long range plan does not exist, what the lack of this strategic document tells you about the group's management.

 *Accreditation Documents.* Governmental and professional accreditation organizations evaluate many tax–exempt institutions, including colleges, museums, and healthcare organizations. These bodies collect voluminous documents on the operations of each nonprofit to ensure that it meets the minimum standards the body prescribes. Many times, board leadership is interviewed as part of the information gathering process — interviews that can be very helpful to your assessment efforts

*The Internet.* There are at least two sites on the Internet that provide information about individual nonprofit organizations, including the chairperson of the board and the executive director:

### http://www.give.org

The National Charities Information Bureau's (19 Union Square West, New York, NY 10003; phone orders: 212/929–6300) site sells very thorough reports about hundreds of nonprofits for $9.95 each. Not only does each report provide information about the group's activities, finances, and governance and staffing, it also evaluates the organization and tells you if it meets the NCIB's standards.

### http://www.bbb.org

On the home page of the Better Business Bureau's site, select "Check a National Charity Report." Select an organization and you'll get a pretty thorough scoop on its programs, governance, fund raising activities, and financial condition. You'll also be told whether it meets the Council of Better Business Bureau's "Standards for Charitable Solicitations." Included in each free, online report is full contact information for reaching the organization.

## ADJUNCT BOARD SERVICE OPPORTUNITIES

As suggested earlier, many boards of directors reserve membership only for certain individuals whose prominence on the corporate, philanthropic, or social scene is quite well established. These directors represent a level of achievement or social position that reflect the image the organization wishes to project. There was a time when these major organizations were satisfied with the status quo and their posture of exclusivity. With few exceptions, those same institutions today are more conscious than ever before of the necessity to incorporate pluralism and cultural diversity into every facet of their operations. Many nonprofits have achieved this goal without abandoning the "standards" used to select their board members by establishing non–governing advisory councils, donor clubs, and docent groups. Many of these adjunct groups also serve as candidate pools for future board prospects as well, but mostly they provide the organization with a level of volunteer participation that effectively extends their reach into its various constituencies.

In general, the larger and more established the nonprofit entity, the more likely it will have adjunct volunteer groups. For example, a well–established art museum may have a "Junior Board" composed of younger business professionals with an interest in art. It may also have a "Founders Society" made up of people who have contributed $1,000 or more to the museum. A large hospital system may have an "Area Council" comprised of business and community representatives who live in the hospital's general service area, and an "Auxiliary Association" that raises funds to purchase medical equipment and for special projects. A major social service agency may have a "Corporate Leadership Council" involved in a capital campaign and a "Gala Benefit Committee" that utilizes the time and energy of dozens of volunteers.

From the standpoint of career transition, participating in these adjunct board groups can often prove to be as valuable as serving on the board of directors. They provide a vehicle for affiliation where the direct board route is not a viable or immediate option. Opportunities for adjunct board service are often numerous with large and prominent nonprofit organizations. Once you have established yourself in one of these adjunct groups, the doors to higher level volunteer responsibilities often open more easily.

## UNITED WAY LOANED EXECUTIVE PROGRAM

If you have worked in a large corporation, you probably have been approached to join the annual local United Way campaign in which contributions to the United Way are deducted regularly from your paycheck. You may have noticed that many of the United Way staff are business professionals working for the United Way as a "Loaned Executive." Many corporations, such as IBM, have adopted the *Loaned Executive Program* in which selected business professionals participate in a paid "sabbatical" while working for a nonprofit organization. The Loaned Executive Program could be a valuable Strategic Volunteering experience for you.

Most corporations that participate in the Loaned Executive Program have developed criteria for selecting employees to participate. The criteria can be part of the grooming process for young professionals on their way up the corporate ladder or it may stand alone as a personnel function through which you can apply for the position. People have been selected for other reasons including when an employee's job is about to be eliminated or because an employee is close to retirement. Ordinarily, the people selected as Loaned Executives are valued employees who will return to their company job when the United Way experience is over. Although the length of service varies, it is usually runs for about a year. Loaned Executives receive their normal salaries. In some instances the United Way pays for part or all of the

Loaned Executive's salary, although it obviously prefers that the participating company underwrite the cost of compensation.

Loaned Executives are responsible for raising money, usually from corporations and foundations, through the analysis of corporate portfolios, preparing and delivering personal presentations to corporate executives, and planning fund raising  efforts. The United Way wants people for this program who like to raise money. If your nonprofit career transition goal includes fund–raising, the Loaned Executive Program is an excellent strategic experience to pursue.

# Networking In the Nonprofit Sector

While most people think of networking as a job–search tool, you consciously or unconsciously use networking principles every day as you develop your business career and as you expand the scope of your personal business contacts. You get to know people throughout your company and at other companies, at social gatherings, and in professional activities. You identify and develop these connections, and build upon them for different purposes, at different times, and with different levels of intensity and frequency. This network represents linkages with people, who are connected to each other through a vast array of social, business, and personal ties. This linkage is the reason networking works so well for locating new job opportunities. Everybody knows someone who knows somebody, and the last "somebody" could be your next employer. It happens every day and it is regarded by many as one of the most effective ways to find a new job.

Networking takes on two additional dimensions when you make the career transition to the nonprofit world. On the plus side, nonprofit organization professionals are incredibly helpful when it comes to building your network of contacts. In as much as charities represent helping organizations, professionals who work for them are motivated by their desire to be helpful to others. This mind set is pervasive and nearly uniform. Unlike the business sector, you will rarely find a nonprofit professional who is too busy to talk with you or who will not take the time to refer you to someone else.

On the negative side, the linkages and connections you have cultivated and maintained in your business life are not with people who are going to hire you in the nonprofit sector. It is a completely different network. However, the dynamics involved in networking allow you to use your business contacts to initiate your nonprofit referral network when you have no other place to start. It is always a good idea to tap your business contacts first to initially identify your nonprofit networking opportunities. If this sounds confusing or even contradictory, let me try to clarify.

## MAKING THE MOST OF YOUR BUSINESS CONTACTS

Your current employer offers the most accessible environment for utilizing your business contacts. Earlier I noted that 56 percent of the adults in this country volunteer their time to nonprofit organizations. If you work in a company with 2,000 employees, there are probably at least 1,000 among them involved with at least one nonprofit — a wealth of opportunities to begin building your nonprofit network! Even if you work in a small company, at least half of your co–workers are probably affiliated in some way with a charitable organization — a ready–made starting point for information gathering and personal referral potential.

The fun of networking is that the networking path often leads to the unexpected. For example, a management consultant for a major accounting firm was having a lot of difficulty getting to the "movers and shakers" in the private conservation field, the object of his nonprofit transition strategy. A casual remark made by one of the secretaries one day led to an introduction to her father–in–law who sat on the board of one of the largest endangered species organizations in the country. Today that management consultant works as the controller of a wildlife research institute — thanks to the father–in law introducing him to that organization's CEO. Your co-workers may represent a wealth of personal contacts in the nonprofit sector. You may miss out on a significant link that is right under your nose if you fail to build a nonprofit network where you currently work.

Use any of the following questions in casual conversation with your coworkers to identify potential nonprofit networkers where you are currently employed:

- ❑ Are you a volunteer with any charities in this area?
- ❑ Is your spouse (or significant other) involved in any nonprofit activities?
- ❑ Who in our company does a lot of charitable work?
- ❑ Do any of your close friends serve on the board of directors of any nonprofit organization? Do any of them work for a nonprofit?

☐ What about your brothers and sisters? Are any of
them involved in charitable work in this area?

The beauty of developing and using your business
network in your nonprofit job search is that you can ask
these sorts of questions entirely in the open. As far as
anybody can tell, you're just looking to make contacts so
you can find a worthy organization for which you can
volunteer. It does not require the element of confidentiality in your information gathering that a search in the
business sector warrants. As a result you are not limited
in your investigation and research of opportunities, because your coworkers and even your boss will think you
are interested in volunteering and that you want to meet
people who work in such nonprofit organizations.

Another source of nonprofit organization information
that may exist at your current employer is your corporate contributions or public affairs manager. Many
larger companies have an annual procedure for identifying and selecting charities to receive tax deductible do-
nations. Many corporations have established foundations for this purpose and donate cash and in–kind
contributions such as business equipment, products
the company manufactures, supplies, and services. You
can ask the person in charge of charitable contributions
for a list of organizations the company supports and the
amount of support it provides. This information is an
important part of your network building for two reasons.
First, it is likely that if the company makes a donation to
a certain charity it may also have company employees
who serve as volunteers or board members for that charity. These people are excellent contacts that you should
bring into your new nonprofit network. Second, whether
or not your employer does more than make cash contributions to an organization, this link is often enough of a
connection to enable you to directly contact the organi-

zation's chief executive officer, a level of contact at which you ultimately want to focus most of your networking activity and energy.

Finally, your professional relationships with outside business clients and customers, your major suppliers, vendors, contractors, and everyone else who does business with your employer offer a possible link to the nonprofit world. Even the worker who delivers your bottled water may be a key link in your networking to nonprofit employment. Never assume that the perceived status of a person's job is an indication of his or her ability to help you, particularly where the nonprofit sector is concerned. Your network building objective at the very start is to gather as much information on nonprofit contacts as possible, from your co–workers, clients, customers, and others. From there you can begin to assess the significance of those connections in relation to your ultimate nonprofit employment objectives. While this effort is time consuming, it is an invaluable process particularly if your nonprofit network is limited.

## REACHING THE NONPROFIT CEO

The chief executive officer is the key person you want to reach as you begin to refine your nonprofit networking connections. The smaller the organization, the easier it is to reach the executive director. The larger the nonprofit, the more it will seem like trying to reach to the CEO of a giant corporation. Whatever the case, the executive director carries the most influence in the organization and represents the level of decision making that will most likely lead you to suitable job opportunities. This is not to say that department or division heads un-

**SYLVIA**                                    **by Nicole Hollander**

der the chief executive are unimportant as networking contacts. But it is the chief executive of any organization, profit or nonprofit, who has the greatest voice in hiring decisions.

If you have implemented the ideas presented in Chapter 4, "Strategic Volunteerism," to land yourself on a board of directors or adjunct board, you have achieved a significant plateau in your readiness to develop a network of contacts, starting with the chief executive on whose board you serve. She has the ability to introduce you to the right people in similar organizational settings, either formally or informally depending on the appropriateness of the connection.

One of the most effective informal ways of being introduced is at professional meetings, conferences, and conventions of professionals and nonprofit organizations. For example, the American Association of Museums holds a large annual national convention and smaller regional conferences to which many museums send their directors. Attending these gatherings is a productive way to learn about the field's state–of–the–art practices as well as get acquainted with other museum professionals — in other words, to network. The chief

executive of the organization on whose board you serve
will generally be willing to introduce you to his peers in
similar organizations. It is most always helpful to openly
discuss your career transition objectives even though
you sit on her board. This does not in any way represent
a conflict of interest or disloyalty to the organization on
whose board you serve. In most cases the chief executive
will be more conscious of your desires and therefore
more diligent in helping you meet your transition objectives. **Remember:** *Nonprofit organization professionals
want to be helpful; that's why they got into the business
in the first place.*

Fund raising events offer yet another way to meet
chief executives of organizations where you may wish to
pursue employment opportunities. There is hardly a
public charity in existence that does not have at least
one program every year at which its various constituencies come together to raise money for its operations. Organizations with a very high public profile such as symphony orchestras and zoos, and charities where events
typically represent the most cost effective way to raise
money such as the Multiple Sclerosis Society and Special Olympics, may have a dozen or more fund raising
events a year. The executive staff as well as key board
members and often key management staff attend these
events. Your contribution that gets you into these fund
raisers gives you the opportunity to meet and talk with
these top leaders of the nonprofit community .

# SOURCES OF NETWORKING INFORMATION

The most effective contact networks tend to be based
on personal referrals. Let's face it, nothing really tops

face–to–face interaction with someone who can provide job–search insights and who can open doors to job opportunities. But reaching people at that level can be difficult or next to impossible. Still some hard work can open the doors to meet good networking contacts. You can create the opportunity to build your contact network by thoroughly researching documents and printed materials on nonprofits in addition to gathering information from personal interviewing. There are a good number of directories and periodicals that can help you develop your network.

## Annual Reports

Most nonprofits publish a year–end report filled with information on its programs and services. They also include at least lists of staff members as well as the board of directors. Some even include brief paragraphs about each director or staff member. To obtain an annual report, usually for free, just write or call the organization. A growing number of groups post their annual report on their web sites.

A nonprofit's annual report can provide good linkages for your network that can be difficult to discover simply by word–of–mouth. An annual report usually gives the title and employer of each board member. This information can help you identify any directors who may work for the same employer as you do, work for one of your major client or customer accounts, be a member of a professional group or club to which you belong, or serve on the board of directors for another nonprofit group where you have good contacts.

When you need to dig still deeper into a particular nonprofit organization to discover potential network contacts, ask the organization for a copy of its annual reports from three and six years ago. Because many organizations limit the number of terms an individual may serve on their board, these older annual reports will identify members who have left the board — people who can still become a key network connection for you even though they are not currently board members.

## MEMBERSHIP DIRECTORIES

Hundreds of professional organizations serve the different segments of the nonprofit industry. Some are related to specific jobs or professions within a particular charitable segment such as the North American Association of Synagogue Executives and the National Association of College and University Business Officers. Others are related to specific organizational entities, such as the American Association of Botanic Gardens and Arboreta. Whatever their membership focus, these associations share one key thing in common: they publish a membership directory in print and/or online. Most of these directories are available to the general public for a nominal charge.

**KEY RESOURCES**

The most complete compilation of information on directories of professionals who work in the nonprofit sector appears in the *Non-Profits & Education Job Finder* (described on page 174). You'll find detailed information about hundreds of directories of professional's in just about every nonprofit field so you can decide which ones are right for you. For health care, see the *Professional's Job Finder* also described on page 174.

Fortunately, most professional membership organizations are pretty focused — so you can target the associations whose membership directories may help you identify potential networking contacts. It is often helpful to ask the person with whom you are networking what professional membership organizations he belongs to. Ask about the leadership structure within those associations. People who are in professional association leadership roles often have the very extensive contacts within their field.

Often overlooked as a source of helpful networking information is your college alumni directory. There's a good chance that many of your fellow graduates now work in the nonprofit industry. The listing for each alumnus often includes the graduate's current business affiliation and contact information. If this information is not included, you might want to check with your college's development office since it commonly maintains information on its alumni donors that it might be willing to share with you.

## LIBRARIES

Librarians are among the most dependable sources of accurate reference information available anywhere. If a document you need exists, they will almost always find it for you. Unfortunately, in today's world of computer–accessed information systems, libraries are often thought of as the last resort. But most large libraries have access not only to the same computer–accessed information systems you have via the Internet, but they can also access databases that are not available to the general public on the Internet and are prohibitively expensive for individuals to buy or lease. So be sure to visit your local library to find directories of nonprofit organizations and the other types of documents recommended in this chapter.

Special library resources are also available for the nonprofit world. The Foundation Center in New York

City is the hub of a specialized regional library resource network with locations in every state and Puerto Rico. Each "Cooperating Collection," as they are called, serves as a repository of information about private and corporate foundations as well as information about the charitable organizations these foundations support. The Cooperating Collections also contain reference materials, directories, books, and periodicals about entities in the nonprofit sector. For instructions on how to find the Cooperating Collection closest to you, see Chapter 11 beginning on page 165.

Since nonprofit organizations routinely use these special libraries to identify and evaluate the guidelines of various foundations as potential funding sources, these special libraries are good places to informally meet and network with nonprofit professionals.

## Fund Raising Consulting Firms

As the nonprofit sector has grown, an entire industry of related and support services has developed. Fund raising consulting firms constitute one of the fastest growing of these support industries. Just 25 years ago there were only a handful of old–line fund raising consulting firms: Ketchum, Brakeley; American City; Community Counseling Service; and Cargill Associates. As the fund–raising needs of nonprofit organizations have escalated, and competition for corporate, foundation, and individual contributions has grown more intense, many solo–practitioner fund raising consulting firms were born. The marketplace began to fragment with firms of various sizes and specialties so that by the 1980's the industry had been dramatically and permanently changed. Today, there are hundreds of firms across the country that offer a variety of fund raising services to nonprofits.

Fund raising consultants who have been in the business for a while make excellent sources of networking information. In the course of their consulting careers, they frequently interact with the top leadership of nonprofit organizations such the chief executives and the board of directors as well as the key constituent groups that support each organization. They know the strengths and weaknesses, potential and threats to the organization's future, and have a good picture of the employment opportunities in the different segments of the nonprofit industry.

It is crucial that you approach fund raising consultants with a great deal of tact and patience. Confidentiality requirements will prohibit most reputable firms from divulging sensitive or proprietary information about their clients. Initially, a consultant may hesitate to tell you very much about a client organization, but be persistent. While you should respect a consultant's need to maintain confidentiality, also recognize that, by definition, consultants help people.

Most states require fund raising consulting firms to at least register with the state. Contact the state agency responsible for business licensing to obtain a listing of such firms in your targeted geographic area. See Chapter 9, beginning on page 152, for a brief directory of fund raising consultant firms.

## USING THE INTERNET

Nonprofit organizations of all sizes are developing web sites to publicize their mission and services, distribute information, and hire employees. I will not even attempt to begin listing all the nonprofit web sites that exist or are in the process of being developed. Two "gateway" sites that will connect you to literally thousands of other sites for nonprofits are:

### http://www.philanthropy–journal.org

The **Meta–Index for Nonprofit Organizations** includes links to nonprofit organizations and other "gateway" sites with links to thousands of nonprofit groups.

### http://www.clark.net/pub/pwalker

The **Nonprofit Resources Catalog** located online at  includes nearly 3,000 links to other web sites related to nonprofits and foundations. Many of these links are to sites that offer free online directories of nonprofit organizations.

You'll find details on hundreds more web sites related to nonprofits in the *Non–Profits & Education Job Finder*. For health care, use the *Professional's Job Finder*. See page 174 for details on both resources.

## WORKING WITH SEARCH CONSULTANTS

A relatively small but growing number of executive recruiters focuses on the nonprofit sector. Some of these recruiters work for search firms that concentrate on one nonprofit industry segment, like social services. Others are employed by corporate search firms that maintain a separate and smaller nonprofit practice unit. Over the years, nonprofit search practices have grown primarily because nonprofit executive compensation has reached high enough levels to make search fees attractive. Most retained search firms charge a fee equal to 33 percent of the placed executive's initial annual salary. You will want to research the executive search firms in your area to locate those that maintain a nonprofit practice. See Chapter 8 beginning on page 143 for a thorough directory of executive recruiters for nonprofit organizations.

Having a professional relationship with one or more search consultants who consider your background a good fit for the types of searches they conduct is a decided advantage to you in your job search. There's a good chance that in your business career you have developed such a relationship with at least one corporate recruiter. If so, ask this recruiter if she knows of any nonprofit search consultant to which to refer you. Depending on your relationship with your corporate recruiter, asking him to even introduce you to a nonprofit recruiter would not be an inappropriate request. If you have not worked with a corporate recruiter in the past you will want to focus your efforts on getting to know those nonprofit recruiters who conduct searches in your area of interest. Since this can be a daunting task, I'd like to suggest several guidelines to help you make the connection.

Generally, the larger the executive search firm, the more structured its lines of external communication and the more difficult it is just contact a recruiter out of the blue. Regardless of to whom you send your resume at a larger firm, it will usually be routed directly to the firm's research area to be recorded and entered into its resume database. These firms have offices located around the country and many have international sites. All the offices within a firm work off the same database of resumes. Search consultants use this database to identify potential candidates for specific searches they are conducting. Unless your background matches up with a particular current job search, your chances of being called by the recruiter are pretty slim.

Conversely, smaller firms are not as rigidly structured and usually maintain a less sophisticated and smaller database of job candidates. Consequently, your chances of successfully making a cold–call contact with a recruiter at a smaller firm are much better than at a large firm. Try this approach to smaller firms first, and when you have finally connected with the nonprofit search consultant at that firm you can ask her for a referral to a recruiter in a large firm. This cooperation among recruiters for nonprofits may seem counterintuitive to the business professional. But while recruiters for nonprofits compete for client organizations to hire them, they do not compete for job candidates and are quite willing to refer a candidate to another recruitment firm when they don't have any suitable positions for a candidate.

Naturally you are best off if you develop a relationship with a recruiter who specializes in your area of nonprofit interest. This does not imply that all nonprofit recruiters specialize in a certain practice area, but there are those that do because the firm itself serves a niche market. I previously suggested that one of your networking strategies should include contacting the CEOs of nonprofit organizations that match your primary transition interest. It is likely that such CEOs are already in the databases of many nonprofit recruiters. In fact, a nonprofit recruiter might have placed that CEO in his current job. Having that CEO introduce you to her recruiter is also a viable strategy for connecting with the right firm.

# Chapter 6

# Resumes and Cover Letters for Nonprofit Jobs

You may be surprised to learn that resumes did not become common in the business world until the late 1940s. Fifty years ago, employees typically stayed with the same employer for ten, 15, or 25 years and longer. When an individual sought a new job, it was customary to convey his experience in a letter to a potential employer. These letters followed no particular format and were often poorly constructed and rife with omissions. The curriculum vita, established as the customary summary of an individual's credentials in higher education, eventually became the model for resumes in the business sector, albeit not nearly as lengthy as an academic's vita.

Through the years, the resume, along with the cover letter, has become an essential component of the job application. If you want to test how common the resume has become, see how many of your colleagues do not have one. Not only would you be in a very minuscule minority if you did not have a resume, you might also be a little suspect in the eyes of your peers.

# THE RESUME MYSTIQUE

Resume preparation has also become a bit of an art form. Resume–writing manuals crowd the shelves in the career section of book stores. For better or worse, certain "rules" of resume preparation have evolved to the degree that, upon inspection, a "good" resume can be distinguished from a "poor" resume. Unfortunately, judgments regarding an individual's qualifications for a job are sometimes affected by the way the resume "looks." Compare a typewritten resume with one prepared with a word processor or a resume–writing software application with bold headers, clean lines, bullets, and an attractive layout. How often have you heard someone say: "You can tell a lot about a person just by how their resume looks." Right or wrong, this is a popular perception that has set the norm for resumes. To disregard this phenomenon is to buck a very rigid system.

Your resume is a basic tool of written communication. It allows you to describe in summary fashion, and with great selectivity, your professional qualifications to help convince an employer to consider you for employment. While an attractive resume may make a positive initial impression, good looks alone do not result in a job offer. What matters most is what you communicate about your accomplishments to a prospective employer, how you describe your background, your job responsibilities, the functions and skills you highlight as part of your qualifications, and the aspects of your work on which you decide to focus. These become the critical elements in drafting a resume that effectively communicates your qualifications.

# The Problem with Business Resumes

Making the transition from the business sector to the nonprofit world presents some interesting challenges when it comes to resume preparation. First, your career track, the sum of your background and experiences in the business sector, may translate poorly into your career objectives in the nonprofit sector. For example, if you had ten years of experience as an commercial architect and you were interested in working for an human rights organization, little if any of your architectural background might be relevant to that organization. If you don't produce a very different resume when applying for jobs in the nonprofit sector, your architecturally-oriented resume would probably quickly land in the proverbial circular file.

I met with a 31 year–old compensation analyst for a prominent consulting firm who was having difficulty convincing nonprofit executives of her qualifications to work for a charity. Most employers took one look at her resume, which described her salary management background, and gave her the arched eyebrow and a polite dismissal. While few nonprofit settings actually have a compensation analyst position, she was really interested in doing something very different. Therein lay the problem. Her business resume translated poorly to non-profit opportunities.

A second difficulty with business resumes submitted for jobs in the nonprofit market is the "language" barrier. For example, if you had spent the last ten years as an investor relations representative for a large corporation and wanted to pursue a fund raising job at a major university, your resume would have to capture more of the people–oriented activities you performed as opposed to the financial expertise required as an investor relations specialist. This can be difficult to do.

I once met with a 42 year–old mortgage banker who was seeking a fund raiser position at a social service organization. At the top of his resume, in bold type, was the following under a "Summary" of his experience:

| | |
|---|---|
| **Debt Placement** | **Client Development** |
| **Direct Lending** | **Land Sales** |
| **Equity Placement** | **Marketing** |

These areas of responsibility are legitimately important aspects of his 15 years in the mortgage banking business. And the personal skills he possesses in order to carry out these responsibilities (his communication expertise, a talent for nurturing relationships, knowledge of behavior patterns of wealthy individuals) are abilities that might make him a good fund raiser for a nonprofit. These personal qualities represent an important part of his background and experience, yet they are not reflected in his resume. Instead, his business resume barks "Debt Placement" and "Equity Placement" as his qualifications. *These terms are language barriers.* Even if the chief executive of the nonprofit organization knew what equity placement was, it would have little relevance to the charity or to any job opportunities with it.

In addition, some nonprofit executives are often skeptical of business professionals who want to work in the nonprofit sector. A resume that outlines significant accomplishments in business service only reinforces the skepticism. The nonprofit executive will be forced to try to figure out how those accomplishments may practically apply to her organization's mission and program objectives. Compared to an individual who has a nonprofit track record, the business resume simply does not make the connection for the reader. It does not translate business experience usefully and this raises the level of skepticism among nonprofit hiring personnel.

# THE NONPROFIT RESUME FORMAT

Preparing a resume for jobs in the nonprofit sector requires a different approach that presents more of *who* you are than of *what* you are.

There is an old story that says if you wanted to know as much as you could about a person you just met and could ask only one question, what would it be? Somebody from the East would ask, "Where did you go to school?" Midwesterners inquire, "Where did you grow up?" And folks from the West Coast ask, "What's your sign?"

Whatever question you might pose, *who* you are is generally of more interest to people than *what* you are. Obviously, *what* you are in terms of your job title, your status in your company, and your current scope of responsibility are not unimportant. But when it comes to making an impression in the nonprofit world, your personal attributes, namely *who* you are, are what nonprofit executive first assess about your suitability for employment. This orientation reflects the values and culture of the nonprofit sector. Describing *who* you are begins to

> ## Nonprofit Language Practices
>
> **People in the nonprofit sector tend to be sensitive about terms that many may consider to be sexist. For example, you would be most prudent to use in your resume terms like "Chairperson" or "Chair" rather than "Chairman," and "Spokesperson" rather than "Spokesman."**

answer any questions about your motivation to work in the charitable sector. Talking about who you are tends to remove skepticism about why you are making the transition.

In most situations, focusing on yourself as a business professional is going to derail your transition to the nonprofit organization. Trying to rewrite your business resume to fit nonprofit opportunities, even for those job positions that may be similar to your background, is often difficult and can still be inadequate once re–tooled. So, when preparing your nonprofit resume, put your current business resume aside.

The nonprofit resume format I recommend for business professionals in transition does not resemble the traditional chronological resume format. But the information contained in it will be more familiar and comfortable to the nonprofit employer than any revision of your current resume. This new format consists of four distinct components, each of which plays a unique part in communicating who you are and the value of your background to a nonprofit organization. These components also directly relate to the transition strategies presented in this book. In effect, the nonprofit resume is the product of your assimilation experience, the recognition of your transferable skills, your strategic volunteerism, your NPPI index factoring, and your nonprofit organization networking. The five components of your new nonprofit resume, in order, are:

| IF YOU HAVE A B.A. OR ADVANCED DEGREE: | IF YOU HAVE A TWO-YEAR DEGREE OR NO DEGREE: |
|---|---|
| 1 Educational Background | 1 Community Involvement |
| 2 Community Involvement | 2 Transferable Skills |
| 3 Transferable Skills | 3 Your Business Brief |
| 4 Your Business Brief | 4 Educational Background |
| 5 Nonprofit References | 5 Nonprofit References |

Don't let the "One Page Rule" so common in business resumes restrict your nonprofit resume. From my own experience, the resumes within the nonprofit arena are usually two or three pages long for applicants with ten or more years work experience. There is really no preferred number of pages that yields a "good" nonprofit resume. With this understanding, you can feel free to articulate your qualifications without regard to these mythical page limitations.

Begin your resume with your name, address, and the phone number or numbers at which you wish to be called. Be sure to specify which number is for your home and which is for your work phone number.

The rest of your nonprofit resume includes the five components that follow. The order in which you present these sections depends on how much education you have completed, as is explained in the section on educational background that follows immediately.

## EDUCATIONAL BACKGROUND

Nonprofits generally place a high value on education. It is not unusual for job postings to indicate a requirement for a bachelor's degree and preference, if not requirement, for a master's degree. Very few of these positions require a terminal degree. In my experience, nonprofit job candidates are more marketable with two masters degrees than with a Ph.D., except in organizations that focus on education. In addition, a job candidate who pursues continuing education opportunities in her chosen field seems to have more appeal in the nonprofit marketplace. Scholarships, awards, academic honors, and relevant extracurricular responsibilities are also valued.

Present your educational achievements in a manner that will make the most favorable impression. If you have a bachelor's degree indicate the specific degree, major concentration, college or university with its location (city, state), and the year in which you received the degree. Also include any awards or honors you received at the institution. Place this information at the top of your resume. If you have a master's degree, specify the same information and place it first in order above the bachelor's degree. If you have two master's degrees, list them in reverse chronological order at the beginning of your resume.

If you have a terminal degree such as a Ph.D., J.D., or medical degree, list your academic achievements at the top of your resume beginning with your bachelor's degree and ending with your terminal degree. Unless your terminal degree directly relates to the nonprofit management position you are seeking, this subtle difference in presenting your doctorate will generally make a more positive impression. This is not to contradict the fact that nonprofits place a high value on educational achievement nor is it meant to denigrate this accomplishment. The issue is one of perception and relevance. In many instances, your terminal degree can label you as "overqualified." And a terminal degree may not be relevant to the skills you need for the nonprofit management opportunity for which you have applied. The approach suggested here enables you to de–emphasize your terminal degree while still allowing you to include it in your nonprofit resume.

If you attended a college or university but did not receive a degree, or if you received only an associate degree or a technical school degree, do not put this information at the top of your resume. The best place to present these accomplishments is after your Business Brief where it will appear to be more relevant. This is also true of content–specific business certifications you may have acquired such as a real estate or brokerage license. If you place all educational information not relevant to the nonprofit sector after your Business Brief, it will receive the proper recognition by the nonprofit reader.

## Community Involvement

Most business resumes include a short section near the end with a cursory listing of the job applicant's community service or volunteer experience. Generally, the name of the nonprofit organization is listed as well as any professional or community associations in which she has been active.

This is fine if you are seeking job opportunities in business. But when making the transition to the nonprofit sector, your community involvement and volunteer experiences are a key part of your background that needs to be presented in more detail than in a resume for a business or government job. To emphasize it, you need to place your community service near the beginning of your resume. But simply listing the names of organizations for which you have volunteered is inadequate and will not enhance your credibility in the nonprofit sector — and the purpose of this part of your resume is to enhance your credibility as a potential employee of a nonprofit organization.

In your transition process, your volunteer activities and responsibilities give you credibility as a job candidate. Consequently, you need to present your volunteer work in more dramatic fashion than in a resume for work outside the nonprofit sector.

Remember, your volunteer activities are productive work. They are not menial, nor superfluous. In the most practical terms, volunteer labor is work for which no tangible compensation is provided. The fact that you are not paid to attend board meetings, or serve on numerous committees, or help organize fund raising events does not make these activities unimportant. We all know successful business professionals (you may be one of them) who put in ten or more volunteer hours per month on various church, civic, and community activities. I doubt that anyone would ever agree that time is not one of their most precious commodities or that their involvement as a volunteer is not worthwhile.

So get your nonprofit resume off to an effective start with a description of your community involvement. This section should be in the same style as your paid employment with the same format as your business resume where you highlight titles, accomplishments, responsibilities, and even promotions. The more involved you are in significant levels of volunteer service, the more detailed your record of volunteer accomplishments should be. These are the principles used in preparing a "good" resume, and it holds true here also. The following examples of descriptions of community involvement should give you a good idea of how to frame your own community involvement experiences.

## COMMUNITY INVOLVEMENT

1986 – 1993     **Williams Bay Family Service Agency**   Williams Bay, New Jersey

Established in 1956, the Williams Bay Family Service Agency is a nonprofit youth and family counseling agency that provides individual, family and group therapy with a budget of $1.3 million and a staff of 40.

**Board of Directors**   Vice President (1990 – 1992)

Chaired the Committee on Accreditation which involved the review and documentation of programs, services, operating budget, public support, and evaluation.

Represented the Agency as a panel member on "The Board's Fiduciary Responsibility" at the Annual Conference of Family Service Agencies.

**Chairperson, Personnel Committee** (1988 – 1990)

Led the effort to review, update, and revise the entire "Personnel Policy Manual" to bring it into compliance with regulations.

Chaired and mediated an employee grievance procedure involving an adverse action which resulted in a mutually satisfactory dismissal arrangement.

1991+ **United Way of the Tri–Cities**   Dalton, Ohio

The United Way of the Tri–Cities serves a population of over 375,000 in support of 22 human service agencies with a $2.2 million annual operating budget.

**Chairperson, United Way Employee Campaigns** (1992, 1993, and 1996)   Dalton Manufacturing Corporation, Dalton, Ohio

Increased employee giving to United Way through improved marketing including video presentations, special fund raising events, and motivational meetings which resulted in increased contributions of:

14 percent in 1992;
29 percent in 1993; and
31 percent in 1996.

Worked closely with United Way staff, outside video consultants and marketing firms in the conception and production of a five–minute motivational video on United Way agencies which has been used successfully in the past four campaigns.

Developed, organized, and coordinated a fund raising event that involved 300 employees and their families resulting in a 200 percent increase in contributions from those who attended.

1985+    **Marymount Wildlife Foundation**  Sandoval, Georgia

A tax–exempt, 501(c)(3) private, operating foundation, Marymount seeks to preserve and protect endangered animals and plant life indigenous to the northern Georgia territory.

1989+    **Charles T. Sanders Society,** Member

Active support of Society which develops public educational materials on endangered animals such as the Red Wolf. Members of the society who contribute at least $500 per year to the Management Wildlife Foundation.

**Business Advisory Council,** Member (1985+)

Attend quarterly meetings to support the Marymount Wildlife Society's Foundation's efforts to encourage business participation in habitat preservation.

Assisted in the development of a major capital campaign to construct a new research wing for the expansion of the flora and fauna research department.

**Trail Guide** (1985 – 1989)

Served as one of 40 volunteers trained and qualified to lead field outings of youths and adults into the Carlson Canyon area as part of the foundation's educational discovery program.

| 1991+ | **American Heart Association of Metropolitan Chicago**   Chicago, Illinois |
|---|---|

The Metropolitan Chicago AHA Chapter is one of the largest in the nation. It provides education, medical research, and public information on the nation's top killer, heart disease.

**Chairperson, Major Gifts Committee**   (1991+)

Lead 22–member committee of volunteers in the design and implementation of a major fund raising program that focuses on donors of $250 and more.

Participated with staff in the selection and recruitment of additional committee members for major gift campaign roles.

Wrote and distributed solicitation mailing to local business and corporate leaders that resulted in increased giving levels.

**Corporate Contributions Committee: Chairperson, New Prospects Task Force** (1986 – 1990)

Initiated first program to expand the number of first–time business and corporate donors in the Chicago area.

Increased the number of new business contributions by 343 percent in three years.

Increased the number of new business sponsors by 190 percent in two years.

# TRANSFERABLE SKILLS

Certain functional skills and most content–specific skills are difficult to translate into the nonprofit environment. The longer you adhere to and perfect certain skills in the business world, the more ingrained they become. So when you get ready to make the transition to nonprofits, you naturally fall back on those abilities you use best. We know that many of the same skills are valued highly in both the business and nonprofit arenas and each of us has developed these abilities in our careers to some extent. This is an important fact when it comes to communicating your background to the nonprofit sector. These perceived skills form the bridge that is a key part of your assimilation experience.

Chapter 2 presented the findings of the McCauley and Hughes study on which skills corporate and nonprofit managers value the most. The results indicated that corporate and nonprofit managers ranked the same three skills at the top of the list: flexibility, resourcefulness, and staff development. These are the skills that both corporate and nonprofit managers recognize as essential to sound management practices. They are also the skills that are the most transferable between the corporate and nonprofit sectors. Recognizing this commonality between the business world and nonprofit sector will help you prepare your new nonprofit resume by providing the important bridge for describing yourself without introducing language barriers.

The second part of your nonprofit resume presents, in jargon–free language, your business skills that are transferable to the nonprofit sector. Use the McCauley & Hughes study as a guide for formatting the presentation of your transferable skills. Describe in some detail your duties and accomplishments from your prior business settings. Those accomplishments do not necessarily have to be in chronological order nor do they need to reflect your career path. In fact, you should format your responses beginning with those abilities that represent the strongest examples of your skills under that category.

For example, Mary Ann has 12 years of business banking experience in the investment arena. Her accomplishments and responsibilities relate well to the three highest ranked McCauley & Hughes management abilities. This is how she described her transferable skills in this part of her resume for nonprofit jobs.

## TRANSFERABLE SKILLS

### Adaptability/Flexibility

Initiate contact with and coordinate professional relationships with corporate executives, foreign banking representatives, financial institutions, and pension fund managers, each of which requires balancing varying concerns and interests, and treating people with respect and professionalism.

Continually communicate bank policies and practices to institutional investors by writing periodic correspondence, phone contacts, and socializing with clients.

Maintain diplomacy and tact in dealing with diverse constituencies of the financial community, balancing sensitivities and providing information often on an immediate basis in order to help others plan and make decisions.

### Resourcefulness/Creativity

Created new marketing literature to familiarize potential and current clients with the bank's services. The entire department eventually adopted this format.

Researched and created an original format for evaluating prospective clients resulting in a new marketing plan approach; also adopted by the entire department.

Reduced departmental expenses by $300,000 without sacrificing the employee group's efficiency or productivity.

## Staff Development/Leadership

Assisted staff of three under my supervision in developing a new approach to customer relations which resulted in a 37 percent improvement in their work.

Planned and annually implemented six social events for customers in coordination with bank staff that represented other departmental areas.

Created and implemented a bi–monthly staff focus group series in which each staff member was given the opportunity to present an issue and lead a discussion on it as a way to improve internal communication and teamwork.

Delegated to staff and assisted staff in the design of new computer spreadsheet applications for reporting monthly trade volume which was later adopted by the whole department.

---

Mary Ann's description of her transferable skills offers three valuable lessons. First, it presents concrete examples of business accomplishments without using business jargon, industry slang, or acronyms that might be unfamiliar to someone in the nonprofit sector. She selected her accomplishments that are most likely to be important in a nonprofit setting and avoids going into a lot of detail on the business operations side. This is a good technique for you to use, particularly if your business background has little to do with the nonprofit field you wish to enter.

Second, Mary Ann has been in a job that requires much sensitivity, tact, diplomacy, trust, integrity, and communication ability — all interpersonal skills highly valued in the nonprofit sector. She has proffered examples of her business accomplishments that relate specifically to nonprofit situations in which she may find herself. The more you know about the nonprofit industry you wish to enter, and the more you know about the specific type of organization you want to work for, the more specific you can be in describing your skills in your nonprofit resume.

Finally, Mary Ann's descriptions of transferable skills focus as much on the *process* of applying her abilities as on their outcomes and her accomplishments. In the business world the bottom line is the bottom line. Results are quantifiable and measurable. In the nonprofit area, the bottom line is not so clear cut. Remember that within the nonprofit universe, process issues are often as important as outcomes. You can make your transferable skills more relevant to potential nonprofit employers by devoting as much of your resume to describing how you've applied your skills as to describing the outcome of your actions.

## BUSINESS BRIEF

Generally speaking, your nonprofit resume does not need to include as many details about your business qualifications as your resume for the business world included. Follow this basic rule in documenting your "Business Brief:"

The more closely your business background parallels the nonprofit jobs you seek, the greater the amount of detail about your business experience and accomplishments should go into your nonprofit resume.

When your business background does not parallel the nonprofit jobs you are seeking, you can use a more simplified listing of your business experience in which you would identify only three aspects of your business background in reverse chronological order:

**1**   The companies you have worked for and their locations,

**2**   The titles of the positions you have held, and

**3**   The dates between which you held those positions.

For example, Wesley has 15 years of experience in sales management in the hi–tech business equipment industry. He is interested in taking his considerable avocational background in coaching youth sports and organizing youth development programs to a full–time career in the youth development sector. Since his business experience does not match his nonprofit interests, his nonprofit resume should include a brief listing of his business background.

| 1990+ | **Matsuata Software, Inc.,**   Newton, CA |
| | Director, National Sales |
| | **Capra Digital Corporation**   San Diego, CA |
| | Regional Sales Manager, 1987–1990 |
| | Marketing Representative, 1985–1987 |
| | Sales Planning Coordinator, 1982–1985 |
| | **Winthrop Computing Company, Inc.**   San Diego, CA |
| | Sales Representative |

In functional terms, some jobs and career tracks in the business sector are the same or similar to some nonprofit sector positions. Many jobs in the financial field that carry titles like controller, business manager, accountant, and accounts payable/receivable require the same functional and experience requirements whether in for–profit or nonprofit organizations. The same holds true for public and media relations as well as editorial and other related communications jobs. Career professionals in general human resource management positions are another example. And as information or systems management jobs have grown in the business sector, so too have they in the nonprofit sector. If your business background falls within any of these functional areas or job titles, your nonprofit resume will be stronger if you simply transcribe the experience in your business resume to this section rather than abbreviate that information in the Business Brief format suggested above.

## Nonprofit References

References serve a vital purpose in the job search process. The most helpful references are people who can attest first–hand to your skills in specific work situations. Former business associates are able to validate and verify information and impressions about the candidate that a potential employer needs to make a hiring decision. References who can comment on your professional abilities are generally those individuals to whom you reported at past jobs. They can also be associates with whom you are currently working or with whom you have previously worked.

But business references can present a dilemma when you are making the transition to the nonprofit sector. The business reference you would unhesitatingly use on

a job search in the private sector is usually able to provide a prospective employer with an evaluation of your
*content–specific* skills. But she may find it difficult to
translate your business accomplishments into the nonprofit environment, rendering her a much less effective
reference than you might wish to give a potential nonprofit employer. While a prospective nonprofit employer
will probably want to talk with your business references,
you want to also offer references from the nonprofit sector who will be able to enhance the credibility of your career transition objectives. But how can you present nonprofit references when you have never been employed in
a charitable organization?

The answer lies in the strategic volunteerism and networking described in chapters 4 and 5. Strategic volunteerism provides a way to gain experience dealing with
specific nonprofit organizational development issues,
program formation, finance, and administration — without actually working for a nonprofit. If you have served
on the board of directors of a nonprofit organization, the
organization's executive director can be a valuable job
reference. He often has a first–hand, working knowledge
of the skills and abilities you applied while serving on
the board. If you have served on a board for more than a
year and have taken on committee responsibilities or
served in as officer, the group's executive director will
probably have worked with you closely enough to serve
as a reference when you apply for jobs in the nonprofit
sector.

In addition, if you serve on more than one board of directors you have the opportunity to use other directors
as references. Senior staff of the organization can sometimes serve as good reference sources as well. If you
served as an organization's treasurer and worked well

for a couple of years with its chief financial officer, you could ask the CFO to serve as a reference for you. Remember that other members of the board of directors are potential references for your nonprofit job applications. Board members who are particularly well–known in the philanthropic community make good references.

Identifying reference sources from your information networking process is a little more difficult to accomplish. Just meeting with a nonprofit director during an informational interview, even if you maintained contact with him for many months, does not make him an effective reference. You must distinguish between those network contacts who are links to other sources and those who are prospects for affiliation. The strength of your affiliation with the organization determines whether you can legitimately ask the director or member of senior management staff to serve as a nonprofit reference for you.

In preparing your nonprofit resume, list the names of your nonprofit references in the body of your resume along with their affiliations, addresses, and phone numbers. The appearance of the names of executive directors, senior management staff, and board members with whom you have served and who may hold influential positions among the philanthropic community give your background more credibility.

# THE COVER LETTER

Just as in the business world, the cover letter that accompanies your resume can be even more important than the resume itself. The cover letter is usually read before the resume. Consequently, your cover letter has to quickly capture the prospective employer's attention and motivate her to read your resume.

If you were seeking a job in the private sector, you might include something like one of the following one-sentence summaries of your experience that give the reader a quick glance at your business accomplishments.

> Dynamic Fortune 100 sales management executive with extensive experience in the high technology business equipment industry.

> Twenty years of managerial experience related to establishing and implementing cost cutting measures, vendor negotiations, sales analysis and feasibility studies.

> Over ten years experience consulting and managing in an environment of technological and organizational change, handling a very broad range of assignments related to customer-oriented service strategy and standards.

But this kind of information won't be particularly useful when you apply for a position with a nonprofit organization because these types of business experience are not very relevant to a nonprofit group. Lacking nonprofit experience to summarize in your cover letter, you are faced with a dilemma. How do you condense your two or three-page nonprofit resume into a short lead paragraph in the cover letter that will get the nonprofit reader's attention?

Fortunately, your cover letter can, and should, be customized for each nonprofit job for which you apply. Your resume is the generic part of your job application — you generally use the same resume for all the jobs to which you apply. But without changing your resume, your cover letter offers an opportunity to communicate more explicitly *who* you are rather than *what* you are. Remember, *who* you are is initially going to be of more interest to the nonprofit employer. It also allows you to specifically highlight those items in your resume that make you a good fit for the particular job for which you've applied.

I'm about to tell you to include information in your cover letter that many of the best books on cover letters recommend leaving out. Their advice is very sound for people seeking jobs in the private sector. It's excellent advice for people with established nonprofit careers. But when you are switching from the private sector to nonprofits, you have to adopt tactics unique to this type of job search. The approach that follows is extremely effective, in part because it breaks many of the rules for cover letters.

An effective way to communicate *who you are* is by describing what is motivating you to make a career transition to the nonprofit sector. This is a simple but basic way to initially present yourself. This is your goal, and it allows the reader to immediately know your motives. The short paragraph should be written in two or three conversational style sentence that identify your specific nonprofit industry interests. Consider the following examples and note particularly the way each states a compelling case for initial consideration.

> "My lifelong avocational interest in conservation and environmental issues leads me to make a permanent career transition to the nonprofit sector. Having enjoyed a successful ten–year career in the banking industry, I would like to use my people skills, financial resourcefulness and knowledge of business operations to successfully

develop programs that preserve and protect our natural resources."

Here the business professional briefly notes his ten years of banking experience. He quickly directs the reader's attention to his "avocational interest." He uses the word "permanent" to underscore his commitment to his transition objective and he notes his key adaptive and functional skills which are highly transferable. He does not mention his day–to–day job duties because they would only distract the nonprofit employer.

> "I wish to apply my nine years of volunteer fund raising experience for cultural and educational organizations to a professional career in development. My accomplishments during the past 12 years in the marketing and communications field, specifically in events management and public relations, have relied on my strong writing and oral presentation abilities, attributes which are required for successful fund raising."

In this second example, the business professional first emphasizes her volunteer leadership background in fund raising to build her credentials in this aspect of nonprofit work. She has decided that fund raising is the career track she wants to pursue and she mentions the two kinds of nonprofit organizations for which she has raised money. Acknowledging a specific focus in development, she is "locking" herself into a functional job category which she realizes will probably eliminate her from consideration of other types of jobs. She makes a stronger case for hiring her by presenting more detail about her prior business duties in marketing and communications which are related to the fund raising field. As discussed previously, there are several functional job categories that are the same in business as in the nonprofit sector, such as finance and accounting. When this

## THREE RULES FOR COVER LETTERS

You would be prudent to apply these three rules when writing your cover letter:

**1** Always identify the broad nonprofit industry segment or charitable field you are pursuing. You may hear arguments against this tactic and you may feel that keeping completely open to any and all possibilities is more effective. But, casting a wider net does not catch more fish if the conditions are not right. Targeting your search to one nonprofit industry segment, even if you have more that one interest area, will focus your job search energy and will result in a more effective presentation of yourself.

**2** The closer your business background is to the segment of the nonprofit industry you are pursuing, the more effective it is to highlight relevant parts of your business background in your cover letter. Conversely, where your professional background is not very relevant to the job for which you are applying, or if your particular nonprofit interests do not relate to your prior business duties, focus the your cover letter more on your personal background.

**3** If you have decided to transition into a particular job function within a nonprofit industry setting, you should be able to support that direction by describing your closely–related prior experience. For example, if you have a finance and business affairs background and this is the sort of job you want in the nonprofit sector, summarize your background and experience in your cover letter.

is the case, the cover letter should reflect more of your business experience in that area.

> "I am seeking a senior management position with a nonprofit organization whose mission embraces my personal commitment to improving the quality of life in our inner cities. My eight years of work experience includes work in both government and business with economic development groups and financial institutions. I recently received my Masters of Urban and Regional Planning from the University of Illinois at Urbana."

This job seeker was a certified public accountant who worked for a well–known public accounting and management consulting firm. The experience he relates to governmental, corporate, financial, and economic development has been as an accountant and a management consultant on numerous client assignments. He does not mention a specific nonprofit industry but he very articulately describes his focus in broad and compelling terms: "improving the quality of life in our inner cities." Because the public accounting function is often viewed as a rather narrow career path, omitting any reference to this in his cover letter avoids the possibility that the nonprofit employer will pigeonhole him as a CPA who is only interested in, and qualified for, an accounting job.

Once you've captured the nonprofit employer's attention, what comes next? The next part of your cover letter should be an extension of your motivational statement that goes further into your personal background. The purpose of presenting certain aspects of your personal background is to create a more open, honest look at yourself. This is not the case when presenting yourself in the business world and is why many business professionals have trouble writing this part of the cover letter effectively.

It's important to remember that one of the strongest reasons people go into the nonprofit sector is to fulfill their sense of altruism. Altruism, in whatever venue it manifests itself, is based on caring. The actions that convey caring are fundamentally communicated through interpersonal relations. Caring people who are comfortable relating to each other in an interpersonal way comprise the nonprofit sector. If you can establish an interpersonal connection first, you will have built the bridge of communication for discussing your business experience in meaningful way later on.

Within this framework, the second part of your cover letter becomes an important way to establish that interpersonal link to the nonprofit world. You are a unique individual with a personal history all your own. Think of yourself this way and use your best writing skills to paint an interesting picture of yourself that supports your transition to the charitable sector.

"The second of four boys, I was born and raised in Columbus, Ohio, where my father was an opthalmologist and my mother volunteered for seemingly every organization that asked her to join. After completing my undergraduate degree at Ohio University, I married my wife, Jean (Raymond), and we settled in Cincinnati where I worked for a mutual fund company. Jean started her career in elementary education and stayed there until 1987 when I accepted an offer at Manufacturer's Bank here in Cleveland. With that move, we bought a house and started a family (Jason, now 4 and Jeremy, 2) and we have become very active in the community. For pleasure, I read a lot of non–fiction (U.S. History), ski, play golf, and run 10K races."

In a short paragraph we know a lot about "Joe the person." That's the point. Note that in his brief biography he mentioned his early business background in the broadest terms possible and he only mentioned his current employer, not his job, as a way to orient the reader to his current environment. The focus is on Joe the person, not "Joe the financial executive." Joe happens to be a former investment analyst for a mutual fund company and is a commercial lender at a national bank. We will find that out in Joe's resume. The cover letter is mostly about his personal background.

You can orient your cover letter to read more like an extension of your motives to make the transition if the circumstances are right — as illustrated by the following example.

"I've loved theater ever since I can remember. I signed up for every high school production. At the University of Wisconsin–Madison, where I graduated with a Bachelor of Fine Arts degree and Master of Business Administration degree, I worked theater productions in the summers and volunteered nights in community productions. After graduation, a major airline recruited me as a marketing representative and I have been promoted three times in the past six years. I continue to perform with community theater groups as time permits. My husband of two years, Brian, has an arts background as well. We have made Chicago our home and I enjoy all of the arts, international travel, and antique collecting."

Beth's business resume is solid evidence of her marketing skills with the airline company. She got on a fast track in sales and then was moved to strategic planning and then back into sales nationally. Her accomplishments have been notable. If she wanted to stay in her marketing career she would have a lot of doors still open to her. But Beth wants to work in a community theater as a managing director or producing director. Her cover letter immediately positions herself in this direction. Because most nonprofit theater groups would see her marketing background as useful, she does not hesitate to expand on this part of her business background. Beth has successfully used her cover letter to build her credentials in the theater world.

# Compensation In the Nonprofit Sector

Often characterized as an industry quite distinct from the corporate business sector, the "Third Sector" is a field with a far different set of motives and objectives, and with a purpose very different from that of the business world. The compensation issue makes this distinction abundantly clear.

In the business world, the reward structure is driven by the profit motive. In the nonprofit universe, the service motive drives the reward structure. In business, management reward practices are manifested primarily through monetary incentive systems. In nonprofits, management reward practices are evidenced through various methods of personal recognition and rank. The

*Non Sequitur* reprinted by permission of the Washington Post Writers Group.
Copyright © 1996. All rights reserved.

common sentiment, "I'm not in it for the money," is never more true than in the nonprofit industry. If said in a business setting, you would be considered unbalanced — and that's just the polite term for how most of your colleagues would react.

The fact that people enter the nonprofit sector for reasons other than monetary reward defines the value basis on which nonprofit compensation is buttressed. The proverbial tradeoff that most business professionals initially face in transition to the nonprofit sector is a common dilemma: the chance to pursue greater personal satisfaction and a more meaningful career rather than collecting greater earnings potential and material rewards. Not that nonprofit professionals take a vow of poverty — most would admit that would be ludicrous. But in the nonprofit sector, through its fiduciary responsibility to its donors and key constituencies, and through its self–perpetuating altruism and the public trust it holds, organizations design compensation programs that are compatible with their charitable purposes and that are competitive within their particular nonprofit field.

The great majority of nonprofit organization executives do not earn six–figure salaries with substantial fringe benefits. And because the chief executive's salary establishes the top of the pay scale in the organization, most career positions in the nonprofit sector cannot compete monetarily with those in the business sector.

Having made the decision to pursue a career transition to the nonprofit industry, you no doubt have already pondered the implications of a change in salary and benefits. You have realized that you may have to take a pay cut. In my experience, the longer your career in the business sector and the higher the management level you have achieved, the more likely it is that you will be paid less in the nonprofit sector. The burning question then becomes, "How much of a salary reduction will you face?" The practical considerations of supporting a family or maintaining a lifestyle to which you have become accustomed are very real factors to weigh against the strength of your transition motives and desires. Only you can determine where the balance falls between these two often competing factors.

Understanding the compensation practices of the nonprofit sector will help achieve this balance. How do the compensation standards in the business sector actually compare to the nonprofit world? How do you determine the value of your business experience to the nonprofit marketplace and, therefore, the worth of your background in terms of salary? To what extent can you negotiate compensation when profit objectives are eliminated?

# BUSINESS AND NONPROFIT PAY STANDARDS COMPARED

The nonprofit world is a very segmented job market in which differences in organizational missions, programs, service delivery objectives, organizational size, and location create a patchwork of potential career opportunities. Not surprisingly, these circumstances produce a highly fragmented compensation picture as well, not only within the charitable industry as a whole but even within specific segments of the industry. Some portions of the nonprofit world are notorious for practices that pay well below business–world standards, and in some cases, below nonprofit norms. Others actually pay salaries comparable to equivalent positions in the private sector.

You can generally predict which side of this compensation fence specific nonprofit industries fall by assessing a nonprofit's five key organizational factors:

1. Mission,

2. Total assets,

3. Annual operating budget,

4. Number of full–time employees, and

5. Geographic location or service area.

In practice, the larger the organization, the more it pays. And, as in the private sector, certain segments of the nonprofit field pay better than others. For example, a managerial position with a small arts organization is likely to pay less than a comparable position with a small health care group.

It is also difficult to compare salary information because many jobs in the nonprofit sector, such as fund raising positions, simply do not exist in the business world. The private sector has no equivalent for the nonprofits' professional development officer — the contemporary term for executive fund raising staffers — even though the attributes of sales and marketing positions are highly transferable to fund raising for nonprofits. Compensation for these positions also covers the spectrum, depending on the particular nonprofit industry they are in. For example, fund raisers for social service agencies tend to be paid less than their counterparts at colleges and universities.

To find salary surveys on nonprofits, particularly for the different nonprofit industries, see the *Non–Profits & Education Job Finder* discussed on page 174; salary surveys for health care are listed in the *Professional's Job Finder* which is described after the *Non–Profits & Education Job Finder*.

Today the Internet offers quick and easy access to the results of salary surveys within both the nonprofit and private sectors. Some of the most helpful web sites for anyone seeking information on salaries and benefits are described immediately below.

*When entering these addresses in your Internet browser, be sure to type in "http://" without the quotation marks immediately before each web site's URL (address).*

### www.dbm.com/jobguide

*The Riley Guide* offers links to many web sites that offer information on compensation. Select "Salary Surveys" from the home page to get started.

## jobstar.org

*JobStar,* formerly known as *JobSmart,* links you to over 300 salary surveys from throughout the country. Site–meister Mary–Ellen Mort may have assembled the largest collection of links to salary surveys anywhere on the World Wide Web. Select "Salary Info." Then, under "Profession–Specific Salary Surveys," you'll find "Nonprofits," "Social Work," "Education," and "Health Care," as well as numerous purely private sector occupations.

## erieri.com

The *Economic Research Institute* offers links to over 200 compensation surveys for the U.S. and Canada. Select "Salary, Col, Benefits Surveys/Services" and allow a few minutes for this lengthy list of surveys to load into your web browser.

## www.idealist.org

The group *Action without Borders* offers links to 20,000 nonprofits in 140 countries. Included are links to salary surveys as well as thousands of job listings. You can subscribe to a free daily email newsletter with job listings.

## careers.wsj.com

The *Wall Street Journal's National Business Employment Weekly* offers links to numerous salary surveys by industry, including the nonprofit field. On the home page, select "Toolkit" and then "Salary Data by Industry."

## www.shrm.ors

The *Society for Human Resource Management* offers a solid, albeit short, list of links to compensation surveys. Select "HRLinks."

## www.abbott–langer.com

While this site doesn't offer any significant links, it gives you key details about the two extremely comprehensive salary and benefit surveys that *Abbot–Langer & Associates* conducts each year. The first survey, *Compensation in Nonprofit Organizations,* covers thousands of positions in 95 job categories. The second, *Compensation of CEOs in Nonprofit Orgnaizations* is a subset of the larger survey. You can request a catalog of its surveys by contacting Abbot–Langer by calling 708/672–4200 or writing to 548 First St., Crete, IL 60417.

**pw1.netcom.com/~tomb/recruitment/salaries.htm**

*Tom's Recruitment Directory* offers links to online surveys for 25 fields, including nonprofits.

# Determining the Value of Your Business Experience

Chapter 2 on transferable skills pointed out that the functional abilities that both business managers and nonprofit managers rated "highly desirable" are also the skills most relevant to your transition objectives. They are valuable because they are apropos to undertaking the kinds of responsibilities and activities you would find in the nonprofit sector. In addition, many content–specific skills practiced in the business sector are not relevant to much of the nonprofit world. However, in those cases where content–specific skills fit the requirements of a particular nonprofit job, competitive compensation usually follows. When considering the value of your business skills in the nonprofit sector, and therefore the level of compensation that might be expected, relevance becomes the key factor. The more relevant your business experience is to the nonprofit job you are seeking, the more valuable your business background becomes, and the more likely it is that the compensation level will be competitive with the private sector.

For example, Craig worked as a regional sales representative for a major computer manufacturer after receiving a bachelor's degree in general business four years earlier. He was being compensated quite well. His annual base salary and bonus totaled $52,000. In college he was a popular student; he had an very outgoing personality and a likeable manner. He had become an active alumnus which sparked his interest in the vacant Director of Corporate and Foundation Relations position. Craig talked to the Vice President for Institutional Advancement about the job. Both realized that the functional and adaptive skills used in professional sales and professional fund raising were very closely related. In sales, as in fund raising, you need a good personal presentation style, you must be articulate, and you need good cultivational and follow–up skills. The transferability of Craig's skills was quite natural and he accepted the position for a starting salary of $50,000 which was at the top of the starting salary range for that position.

Content–specific business skills associated with jobs in finance and accounting are among the most relevant to the nonprofit world. Nonprofits usually can match the private sector's compensation levels for finance and accounting positions at the middle–management level and below. For upper–management positions such as chief financial officers, larger nonprofit organizations are more likely to offer salary and benefits comparable to similarly–sized businesses.

Amy held a MBA in finance and economics along with 11 years financial management experience. Her experience included four years in auditing, four as a controller, and the last three as assistant director of finance in charge of several business operations. She was earning $82,000 a year. But Amy and her husband had a two–year old child, her company was going through some dramatic changes, and she felt the need for a major career shift. Through a friend's involvement in charities,

Amy became interested in the nonprofit world. Several months later she interviewed for a chief financial officer position with a nonprofit retirement community and nursing home provider that operated facilities in six states. This organization had assets of $185 million with a $34 million annual operating budget — quite a bit smaller than her current company's $2.2 billion in assets and $600 million operating budget. Yet, a suitable match ensued, and Amy was appointed Chief Financial Officer with the nonprofit matching her current $82,000 annual salary.

# DEALING WITH IRRELEVANT EXPERIENCE

On the other hand, when a business professional obviously lacks relevant or transferable skills suitable to the type of nonprofit work he seeks, it's a lot harder to win a salary and benefits package that approaches what he earned in the private sector.

If this describes your situation, the business experience you possess might not be recognized or "counted" toward some degree of equivalent experience in the nonprofit sector, resulting in a detrimental effect on your starting pay. Business professionals who face this problem include:

- ☐ The commercial real estate sales associate who wants to pursue jobs that involve youth and family counseling services.
- ☐ The attorney who represents major multinational companies, but now wants to work in government relations for an art museum.

▢ The database administrator who seeks a position as a meeting and events planner for a professional association.

The fewer transferable skills you have for the position you seek with nonprofits, the more likely it is that you will have to accept a salary cut. If this is the case, the nonprofit employer will have the upper hand in negotiating the compensation level. When addressing these disadvantages, consider the following two factors can increase the chances that your business experience will "count" and you can increase your chances of earning a higher starting salary:

## "Life" Experience Equivalency

Nonprofit executives frequently talk about something they call "life experience equivalency" — a phrase seldom heard in the business world.

Life experience in this context refers to a perceived level of maturity, an assessment of a person's outlook on life, and the nature of her personal experiences. These experiences can translate into transferable attributes that have been acquired through dealing with life situations, relationships, stresses, and problems. In the absence of relevant functional skills, consider your life experiences and identify those situations where your adaptive abilities may closely relate to the skills required in the nonprofit setting you are pursuing.

## Competitive Pay Scales

It is always a good idea to do your homework on the compensation standards for various jobs you are pursuing *before* you apply for a specific position. This is absolutely essential when you are in a job–search situation where you have a lot of experience that is irrelevant to the nonprofit world. You will need to research the available data from competitive salary surveys and other sources to determine what you should be paid for the type of job you are pursuing. Armed with this information, you have the ability to at least establish a baseline on which you can begin to assess and negotiate a fair and reasonable starting salary level that reflects a competitive marketplace.

# UNDERSTANDING SALARY NEGOTIATIONS

Most nonprofit organizations, particularly the larger and older institutions, operate under a compensation or salary scheme that applies to all employees. These plans vary widely in their descriptions and grading of jobs, the establishment of midpoints and pay ranges for various jobs, and the manner in which merit and other increases are recognized. They also differ substantially in terms of how well they reflect current market conditions, how often they are reviewed and updated, and in their complexity. Generally, the larger a nonprofit is, the more

**DISCOVERING FINANCIAL RESOURCES**

You'll be in an even better position to negotiate compensation if you know the nonprofit's financial resources. This information is often easily accessible via the Internet. The NCIB and Better Business Bureau sites described on page 77 provide details on each nonprofit's finances. In addition, visit **http://www.guidestar.org** where Philanthropic Research, Inc. provides, at no charge, detailed balance sheets for thousands of nonprofits. An example is shown on the next page.

formal and rigid its compensation plan will probably be, particularly at the lower– and middle–management levels. However, its salary ranges are more likely to be more competitive. Conversely, the smaller the nonprofit, the less formal its compensation plan will likely be (if it has

Example of a free GuideStar financial data report
on a nonprofit organization.

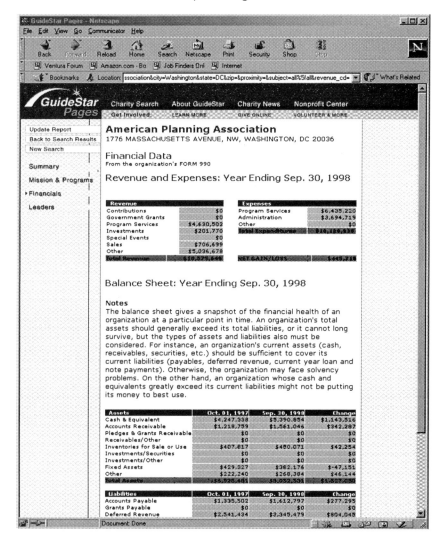

one at all), and the less competitive its compensation practices will probably be.

The relative formality with which a nonprofit compensation plan is administered is a key factor when it comes to salary negotiation. When a nonprofit group must decide whether to go above an established starting salary range to hire the business professional it wants, it bases its rationale on the recognition that the candidate is more highly qualified than all the other applicants even though she is currently paid at or above the established salary. This is an acceptable and common ground on which to negotiate.

In contrast, if your business experience is not strongly related to the nonprofit position you are seeking, negotiating simply on the basis that you are already highly compensated and that you are used to making a certain level of compensation will not get you very far.

As in the business world, there are some types of nonprofit organizations that simply are not willing or able to negotiate:

 A small organization that has relatively few resources;

 A private organization largely funded through government contracts and grants; and

 Lower–level positions at a large organization.

Conversely, the types of nonprofits that are most likely to negotiate with you are:

 An organization where the position you seek is executive director or chief executive officer;

A large organization with formal compensation programs and the position you seek is at a senior management level — this may not be the case at middle– and lower–management levels; and

 A new or emerging organization of any size with an informal or open compensation structure.

# DISCLOSING YOUR CURRENT SALARY

When negotiating a salary and benefits package in the business sector, you are prudent not to reveal your current earnings to your prospective employer. Revealing them may seriously jeopardize your potential for negotiating a better offer. In addition, non–monetary incentives and perquisites can become an important part of the negotiating process.

As you enter the nonprofit world, you will find that the nonprofit world is in stark contrast to the business sector when it comes revealing current earnings. There are a number of solid reasons why, in most instances, revealing your current salary and benefits to a prospective nonprofit employer will actually enhance you chances to maximize your earnings.

First, and most important, the nonprofit culture values openness and directness. Asking for a job applicant's current salary is a common practice among nonprofits. Sharing this information is an important part of the qualifying process. If you won't tell the nonprofit interviewer what your current salary and benefits are, the interviewer could conclude that you do not understand how the nonprofit world operates. This conclusion will not enhance how the employer views your suitability for the position for which you have applied .

Second, the organization's need to remain within budget parameters for designated positions and, in many cases, to respect parity among management positions of similar levels within the organization always affects salary decisions. The organization's knowledge of your current compensation is an helpful benchmark for deciding where you might fit in the group's overall compensation scheme. All too often a nonprofit organization and a business–oriented job candidate go through a series of interviews and establish a mutual interest, only to see the congenial application process fall apart when the job candidate expects a better compensation package than the nonprofit can offer. In the end, both parties walk away thoroughly embarrassed and frustrated.

Third, revealing your compensation always gives you a chance to openly discuss the circumstances surrounding your salary goal. In contrast to the private sector, engaging in a dialogue with the nonprofit organization about your personal obligations and financial responsibilities, within reasonable bounds, is neither strategically incorrect nor inappropriate. This personal information actually helps the nonprofit organization consider your transition situation with more sensitivity, which can make the nonprofit more open to reaching a compensation arrangement that will be more satisfactory to you.

## Two Exceptions

The key exceptions to this advice are when the position sought is the Chief Executive Officer or Executive Director of the organization, or when your compensation far exceeds what the nonprofit organization is willing or able to pay. In these circumstances, divulging a current high salary and benefit package can eliminate you from serious consideration for the job.

I have observed this phenomenon many times. In the nonprofit culture, learning about a job candidate's well-paid status can stir some skepticism among a search committee or interviewer. They begin to wonder how long a highly compensated, successful business professional would stay with us when she is used to making so much more money? When she finds out how demanding and complex the job really is, will she be satisfied earning a fraction of what she earned in the business world?

Regardless of how well you may have presented your transition objectives and motivations, disclosing a current high salary can have a negative psychological effect on the people making the hiring decision — which reflects how the culture of the charitable sector can influence hiring decisions.

Based on my experience, you would be most prudent not to reveal your present salary package if you currently earn 50 percent more than the maximum starting salary of the post for which you've applied. Instead, focus on the value of the position based on such factors as operating budget, size of employee group, and scope of responsibility in a competitive setting. Again, do your homework to learn how the specific industry compensates its chief executives. When the question comes up, address the issue from a philosophical standpoint without being evasive. For example, the following response should be acceptable:

> *"I have been fortunate in my business career to be well compensated for my accomplishments. But*

*that was the private sector and this is the nonprofit sector. I understand the mission of your organization. Based on industry information, I have a pretty good idea of what the going compensation is for a position like this. So, if I am the person you believe is right for this job, I ask only that you consider a level of compensation that fairly represents the marketplace. I fully accept that approach as being the best way to arrive at a fair and workable compensation arrangement."*

The remainder of this book provides resources you can use to implement its advice. Chapter 8 offers a complete directory of firms that recruit executives for nonprofits. In Chapter 9 you'll find a directory of selected consulting firms that conduct fund raising. To illustrate the breadth of opportunities available in association management, Chapter 10 presents of a directory of selected professional associations. Chapter 11 furnishes details on where to find information about charitable organizations. Chapter 12 reports on resources that will help you find a job in nonprofits and facilitate the launch of your new career in the nonprofit world.

# Directory of Nonprofit Recruiters

In Chapter 5 you learned about using executive recruiters in your transition to the nonprofit world. This chapter includes a thorough directory of executive search firms that conduct recruiting for at least one segment of the nonprofit sector. All of these recruiters operate primarily on a retainer basis under which the employer pays the firm for its services. According to *The Directory of Executive Recruiters* published each November by Kennedy Publications (available from Planning/ Communication's "Resource Collection;" see page 176), individuals do not pay fees to search firms. Typically, the employer pays a fee of 33.33 percent of the job's first year salary. Consequently, the search firms are working for their clients, not for you.

*The Directory of Executive Recruiters* reports that an employer engages a retainer firm for a specific hiring assignment, usually to be completed within three to four months. The firm is paid whether or not a satisfactory candidate is found. Typically, the hiring nonprofit uses just one search firm to fill a job opening.

The *Directory* explains that while the recruiter builds a short "slate of candidates" that it seriously considers for the job opening. While you are being considered for a position, no other recruiter at the same firm can contact you for another job even if you are a perfect candidate. This practice makes it unlikely that a recruitment firm will contact you for more than one or two positions within a year.

In addition, the *Directory* explains that if you work for a nonprofit that has retained the search firm during the past year or two, you are considered "off limits" for any other position it may have, even if you are extremely qualified. Consequently, it is very prudent to make yourself known to several search firms when you make your move to the nonprofit sector.

All of the firms listed in this chapter serve the entire United States unless noted otherwise. For additional details, such as contact information for a search firm's other offices, contact the firm or visit its web site.

Again, all of these firms work primarily on a retainer basis and there should be no charge to you, the job candidate. If you discover that any of these firms has moved or stopped serving the nonprofit sector, please let the publisher know by contacting Planning/Communications by email at dl@jobfindersonline.com or by real world mail at 7215 Oak Ave., River Forest, IL 60305. These changes will be posted on the free "Update Sheet" for this book that is available online at URL http:// jobfindersonline.com.

# EXECUTIVE SEARCH FIRMS SERVING THE NONPROFIT SECTOR

## A. T. Kearney, Inc.
222 W. Adams St.
Chicago, IL 60606
Phone: 312/648–0111
URL: http://www.atkearney.com
   Also recruits internationally

## Ast/Bryant
1 Atlantic St
Stamford, CT 06901
Phone: 203/975–7188
URL: http://www.astbryant.com

## Academic Search Consultation Service
Suite 210, 1717 K Street
Washington, DC 20036
Phone: 202/332–4049
URL: http://www.academic–search.org

## Auerbach Associates, Inc.
Suite 400, 65 Franklin St.
Boston, MA 02110
Phone: 617/451–0095
URL: http://www.auerbach–assc.com

## Barnes Development Group, Llc.
Suite 108, 1017 W. Glen Oaks Ln.
Mequon, WI 50392
Phone: 414/241–8468
   Serves only the midwest

## Billington & Associates, Inc.
Suite 900, 3250 Wilshire Blvd.
Los Angeles, CA 90010
Phone: 213/386–7511
   Serves only western states

## Boulware & Associates, Inc.
Suite 1841, 175 W. Jackson Blvd.
Chicago, IL 60604
Phone: 312/322–0088

## Boydon Global Executive Search
Suite 250, 2445 M St., NW
Washington, DC 20037
Phone: 202/342–7200
URL: http://www.boyden.com

## The Burgess Group–Corporate Recruiters International
Suite 6–G, 160 E. 26th St.
New York, NY 10010
Phone: 212/686–5598
URL: http://home.att.net/~burgessgrp
   Also recruits internationally

## C A Durakis Associates
Suite 302, 5550 Sterrett Pl.
Columbia, MD 21044
Phone: 410/740–5590
URL: http://www.durakis.com

**Compass Group, Ltd.**
Suite 460, 401 S. Old Woodward
Birmingham, MI 48009
Phone: 248/540–9110
URL: http://www.compassgroup.com
    Also recruits internationally

**Development Resource Group**
Suite 304, 104 E. 40th St.
New York, NY 10016
Phone: 212/983–1600

**Diversified Search, Inc.**
Suite 3300, 2005 Market St.
Philadelphia, PA 19104
Phone: 215/732–6666
URL: http://www.divsearch.com
    Also recruits internationally

**Educational Management Network, Inc.**
98 Old South Road
Nantucket, MA 02554
Phone: 508/228–6700
URL: http://www.emnemn.com
    Also recruits internationally

**Ferneborg & Associates, Inc.**
Suite 650, 1450 Fashion Island Blvd.
San Mateo, CA 94404
Phone: 650/577–0100
URL: http://www.execsearch.com

**Gahan Associates**
11 Ambrose Ave.
Malverne, NY 11565
Phone: 516/593–3621

**The Hollins Group**
Suite 2121, 250 W. Wacker Dr.
Chicago, IL 60606
Phone: 312/606–8000

**The Hyde Group**
209 Palmer Point R.
Cos Cob, CT 06807
Phone: 203/661–0413

**Jon McRae & Associates, Inc.**
Suite 200, 1930 N. Druid Hills Rd., NE
Atlanta, GA 30319
Phone: 404/325–3252

**KPMG Executive Search**
P.O. Box 31, Commerce Court Postal Station
Toronto, ON M5L 1B2 Canada
Phone: 416/777–8500
URL: http://www.kpmg.ca/
    Also recruits internationally

**Kittleman & Associates, Llc.**
Suite 1710, 300 S. Wacker Dr.
Chicago, IL 60606
Phone: 312/996–1166
URL: http://www.kittleman.net

**Korn/Ferry International**
3232 Lincoln Plaza
Dallas, TX 75201
Phone: 214/954–1834
URL: http://www.kornferry.com
    Also recruits internationally

**Kulper & Company, Llc.**
P.O. Box 1445
Morristown, NJ 07962
Phone: 973/285–3850

URL: http://www.kulpercompany.com
   Serves only the northeast

## Lai Temp Executive Search

Suite 3100, 200 Park Ave.
New York, NY 10166
Phone: 212/953–7900
URL: http://www.laix.com
   Also recruits internationally

## Larsen, Whitney, Blecksmith & Zilliacus, Inc.

Suite 500, 888 W. Sixth St.
Los Angeles, CA 90017
Phone: 213/243–0033
   Also recruits internationally

## Morris & Berger

Suite 700, 201 S. Lake Ave.
Pasadena , CA 91101
Phone: 626/795–0522
URL: http://www.morrisberger.com

## Nordeman Grimm, Inc.

717 Fifth Ave.
New York, NY 10022
Phone: 212/935–1000
   Also recruits internationally

## Opportunity Resources, Inc.

Suite 1017, 25 W. 43rd St.
New York, NY 10036
Phone: 212/575–1688

## Overton Consulting

10535 N. Port Washington Rd.
Mequon, WI 53092
Phone: 414/241–0200
URL: http://overtonconsulting.com

**PriceWaterhouseCoopers Executive Search**
Suite 300, Box 82, Royal Trust Tower, Dominion Centre
Toronto, ON M5K 1G8 Canada
Phone: 416/863–1133
URL: http://www.pwcglobal.com/ca
   Also recruits internationally

**Rob Dey Executive Search**
2869 S. Bumby Ave.
Orlando, FL 32806
Phone: 407/896–6500
URL: http://www.robdey.com
   Also recruits internationally

**Robert Sellery Associates, Ltd.**
Suite 500, 1155 Connecticut Ave., NW
Washington, DC 20036
Phone: 202/331–0090
URL: http://www.sellery.com

**Rusher, Loscavio & Lopresto**
142 Sansome St., Fifth Floor
San Francisco, CA 94104
Phone: 415/765–6600
URL: http://www.rll.com
   Also recruits internationally

**Russell Reynolds Associates, Inc.**
200 Park Avenue
New York, NY 10166
Phone: 212/351–2000
URL: http://www.russellreynolds.com
   Also recruits internationally

**Search Research Associates, Inc.**
85 Tower Office Park
Woburn, MA 01801
Phone: 781/938–0990
URL: http://www.searchresearch.com

### Spencer Stuart
277 Park Avenue, 29th Floor
New York, NY 10172
Phone: 212/336–0200
URL: http://www.spencerstuart.com
 Also recruits internationally

### Stratford Group
6120 Parkland Blvd.
Cleveland, OH 44124
Phone: 800/536–4384
URL: http://www.stratfordgroup.com

### Thomas R. Moore Executive Search
Suite 600, 2000 E. Lamar St.
Arlington, TX 76006
Phone: 817/548–8766

### Tuft & Associates
1209 Astor St.
Chicago, IL 60610
Phone: 312/642–8889

### Wakefield Talabisco Interntional
Suite 8, Menden Meadows, Route 4
Menden, VT 05701
Phone: 802/747–5901
 Also recruits internationally

# Chapter 9

# Professional Fund Raising Consulting Firms

As explained in Chapter 5, firms engaged in professional fund raising often are good targets for business professionals who wish to enter the nonprofit world. This alphabetical directory of fund raising consultant firms should give you a good start.

**Advancement Services Associates and Supplies**

Suite 106, 9431 Westport Rd.

Louisville, KY 40241

502/244–5519

## Alexander O'Neill Haas & Martin
Suite 500, 181 14th St., NE
Atlanta, GA 30309–7603
404/875–7575

## The Alford Group
7660 Gross Point Rd.
Skokie, IL 60077
800/291–8913

## American City Bureau
1721 Moon Lake Blvd.
Hoffman Estates, IL 60194
800/786–4625

## American Support Center
16 Morningdale Ave.
Natick, MA 01760

## Arnoult & Associates Inc.
Suite 315, 2600 Poplar Ave.
Memphis, TN 38112
901/452–8145

## Bachurki Associates, Inc.
303 Seventh St., SE
Washington, DC 20003
202/543–1959

## Baxter Farr Thomas & Weinstein, Ltd.
2238 W. Chew St.
Allentown, PA 18104
610/432–3655

## Carlton & Company
Suite 1900, 101 Federal St.
Boston, MA 02110
800/622–0194

**Carolyn Smith Paschal International**
Suite C–506, 1155 Camino Del Mar
Del Mar, CA 92014
619/587–1366

**Cheney & Company**
20 Grand Ave.
New Haven, CT 06513
203/562–7719

**Community Counseling Service Co.**
Suite 7210, 350 Fifth Ave.
New York, NY 10118
800/223–6733

**Corporate DevelopMint**
#19 Exchange St.
Charleston, SC 29401
803/853–9999

**Demont & Associates**
477 Congress St. 5th Floor
Portland, ME 04101
207/773–3030

**Diane DeMarco**
89 Converse Lane
Melrose, MA 02176
617/665–8120

**The Dini Partners**
Suite 700, 2727 Allen Pkwy.
Houston, TX 77079
713/942–8110

**Divoky & Associates**
50 Salem St.
Lynnfield, MA 01940
617/224–0200

**ADDITIONAL RESOURCES**

*NSFRE Membership Directory* (National Association of Fund Raising Executives, Suite 700, 1101 King St., Alexandria, VA 22314; phone: 703/684–0410) free to members only on the Internet at URL: http://nsfre.org. Lists more than 16,000 members, with contact information. Get membership information at this site. Newcomers to fund raising can join as "Student/Intern" members for up to two years. Call or write for a free copy of NSFRE's *Annual Consultants Directory*.

**The Dockery Group**
1110 Hollybrook Dr.
Wayzata, MN 55391
612/476–0809

**Douglas M. Lawson Associates**
545 Madison Ave.
New York, NY 10022
212/759–5660

**The DuBois Group**
Suite 206, 800 Southwood Blvd.
Incline Village, MN 89509
800/375–2935

**The Edwards Group**
P.O. Box 2176
Terre Haute, IN 47802–0176
812/232–4600

**First Counsel, Inc.**
428 East Fourth St.
Charlotte, NC 28202
800/313–1645

**Foote, Francisco & Co.**
266 Bloomfield Ave.
P.O. Box 430
Caldwell, NJ 07006
800/454–3668

**Fund Consultants, Inc.**
1525 Old Louisquisset Pike
Lincoln, RI 02865
401/729–0100

**Gerald R. Jindra, Inc.**
5306 Sassafras
Cleveland, OH 44129
216/870–3332

**Gershowitz Grant & Evaluation Services**
505 Merle Hay Tower
Des Moines, IA 50310
515/270–1718

**Ghiorse & Sorrenti, Inc.**
Cali Center
50 Tice Boulevard
Woodcliff Lake, NJ 07675
201/307–1970

**Goettler Associates, Inc.**
580 South High St.
Columbus, OH 43215
800/521–4827

**Goodale Associates, Inc.**
Suite 1001, 685 Fifth Ave.
New York, NY 10022
212/759–2999

**Grenzebach Glier & Associates**
Suite 1500, 55 West Wacker Dr.
Chicago, IL 60601
312/372–4040

**GSB Associates, Inc.**
150 South Washington St., Suite 400
Falls Church, VA 22046–2921
703/534–4334

## Hiller Associates, Inc.
6 Water St./Long Wharf
Mattapoisett, MA 02739
800/482–4498

## Hospital Development, Inc.
Suite 32, 11 Hoffman Dr.
Bozeman, MT 59715
406/587–2290

## Jackson & Associates, Inc.
P.O. Box 2827
Evergreen, CO 80437
800/824–8447

## Jeanne Sigler & Associates
500 Fifth Ave., Suite 3600
New York, NY 10110
212/730–4461

## John Brown Limited, Inc.
P.O. Box 29
Peterborough, NH 03458
603/924–3834

## Ketchum, Inc.
Suite 1726, Three Gateway Center
Pittsburgh, PA 15222
800/242–2161

## Mersky & Associates
37 Cedar St.
Newton Centre, MA 02159–1143
617/965–8250

## Phoenix Resources
1830 Sherman Ave.
Evanston, IL 60201
847/475–5100 Ext. 24

**Ruotolo Associates Inc.**
Suite 21, 29 Broadway
Cresskill, NJ 07626
201/568–3898

**Schofield Associates**
Suite 200, 304 W. Franklin St.
Syracuse, NY 13202
800/724–6170

**Schultz & Williams, Inc.**
Suite 400, 421 Chestnut St.
Philadelphia, PA 19106
215/625–9955

**Semple Bixle Associates**
653 Franklin Ave.
Nutley, NJ 07110
201/284–0444

**The Sheridan Group**
2700 South Quincy St.
Arlington, VA 22206
703/931–7070

**Staley/Robeson, Inc.**
3010 Westchester Ave.
Purchase, NY 10577
800/659–7247

**Staley/Robeson/Ryan/St. Lawrence**
Suite 308, 635 W. Seventh St.
Cincinnati, OH 45203
800/883–0801

**The Stanford Group**
211 West 56th St.
New York, NY 10019
212/333–5514

## Thomas R. Conrad & Associates
119 N. 31st St.
Allentown, PA 18104
610/439–1448

## The Thornwood Group
Suite 1900, 101 Federal St.
Boston, MA 02110
617/342–7347

## The Weber Group
Carillon Dr.
Rocky Hill, CT 06067
860/257–3223

## Woodburn, Kyle & Company
400 East First St.
Madison, IN 47250
812/265–6551

# Selected Professional Associations

As a business professional, you probably have joined at least one national, state, or local professional association. These associations can help smooth your career transition path from the private sector to the nonprofit universe. This small collection of selected national professional associations illustrates the breadth of what is available.

**Accountants for the Public Interest**

1012 14th St., NW, Suite 906

Washington, DC 20005

Mildred E. MacVicar, Executive Director

202/347–1668

## American Association of Botanical Gardens & Aboreta
786 Church Road
Wayne, PA 19087–4713
Susan H. Lathrop, Executive Director
215/328–9145

## American Association of Homes for the Aging
Suite 500, 901 E St., NW
Washington, DC 20004–2037
Sheldon L. Goldberg, President
202/783–2242

## American Association of Museums
1225 I St., NW
Washington, DC 20005
Edward H. Able Jr., Executive Director
202/289–1818

## American Association of Zoological Parks & Aquariums
Oglebay Park
Wheeling, WV 26003
Robert O. Wagner, Executive Director
304/242–2160

## American College of Healthcare Executives
840 North Lake Shore Dr.
Chicago, IL 60611
Thomas C. Dolon, Ph.D., President
312/943–0544

## American Hospital Association
840 North Lake Shore Dr.
Chicago, IL 60611
Richard J. Davidson, Executive Director
312/280–6000

## American Marketing Association

Suite 200, 250 South Wacker Dr.
Chicago, IL 60606–5819
Jeffrey Heilbrunn, President
312/648–0536

## American Planning Association

Suite 1600, 120 S. Michigan Ave.
Chicago, IL 60603
Frank S. So, Executive Director
312/431–9100

## American Society of Association Executives

1575 I St., NW
Washington, DC 20005–8825
R.William Taylor, President
202/626–2723

## American Symphony Orchestra League

Suite 500, 777 14th St., NW
Washington, DC 20005
Catherine French, Chief Executive Officer
202/628–0099

## Association for Healthcare Philanthropy

Suite 400, 313 Park Ave.
Falls Church, VA 22046
Dr. William C. McGinly, President
703/532–6243

## ADDITIONAL RESOURCES

For several extraordinarily complete directories of nonprofit associations, see the *Encyclopedia of Associations: National Organizations of the U.S.* and *Encyclopedia of Associations: Regional, State, and Local Organizations*, both published annually by the Gale Group (formerly Gale Research). Together they report on over 125,000 nonprofit organizations in the United States.

Looking for an international position? Check out Gale's *Encyclopedia of Associations: International Organizations.*

All three are available for a fee, online and on CD–ROM under the moniker *Associations Unlimited*. They are expensive, but extremely useful tools for identifying potential employers. Try your library first. To purchase, contact the Gale Group at 800/877–4235, on the Internet at http://www.galegroup.com, and by mail at P.O. Box 9187, Farmington Hills, MI 48333.

## Association of Art Museum Directors
41 East 65th St.
New York, NY 10021
Milicent Hall Gaudieri, Executive Director
212/249–4423

## Association of Science–Technology Centers
Suite 500, 1025 Vermont Ave., NW
Washington, DC 20005–3516
Bonnie Van Dorn, Executive Director
202/783–7200

## Council for Advancement & Support of Education
Suite 400, 11 DuPont Circle
Washington, DC 20036–1207
Peter McE. Buchanan, President
202/328–5900

## Healthcare Financial Management Association
Suite 700, Two Westbrook Corporate Center
Westchester, IL 60154
Richard L. Clarke, President
202/887–1400

## Land Trust Alliance
Suite 410, 900 17th St., NW
Washington, DC 20006–2501
Jean Hocker, Executive Director
202/785–1410

## League of Resident Theaters
Suite 2401, 1501 Broadway
New York, NY 10036
Harry Weintraub, Counsel
212/944–1501

### National Association of College & University Business Officers
Suite 500, 1 DuPont Circle
Washington, DC 20036–1178
Dr. Caspa L. Hams, Jr., President
202/861–2500

### National Parks & Conservation Association
Suite 200, 1776 Massachusetts Ave., NW
Washington, DC 20036
Paul C. Pritchard, President
202/223–6722

### National Recreation & Park Association
3101 Park Center Dr.
Alexandria, VA 22302
R. Dean Tice, Executive Director
703/820–4940

### National Society of Fund Raising Executives
Suite 700, 1101 King St.
Alexandria, VA 22314
Patricia F. Lewis, President
703/684–0410

### National Wildlife Federation
1400 Sixteenth St., NW
Washington, DC 20036–2266
Jay D. Hair, President
202/797–6800

### Wildlife Management Institute
Suite 725, 1101 14th St., NW
Washington, DC 20005
Rollin D. Sparrowe, President
202/371–1808

**ADDITIONAL RESOURCE**

For detailed information on over 250,000 nonprofits, two–thirds of which have budgets over $100,000, see the *National Directory of Nonprofit Organizations* published by the Taft Group (800/877–8238; P.O. Box 9187, Farmington Hills, MI 48333; http://www.taftgroup.com) 6,000 pages in two volumes, published Sept. 1999. It costs $525, so try your library first.

# Sources of Philanthropic Information

## FOUNDATION CENTER COOPERATING COLLECTIONS NETWORK

As noted in Chapter 5, you can discover a wide array of information about nonprofit organizations through the publications available at The Foundation Center and its "Collaborating Collections" network in all 50 states, as well as the District of Columbia and Puerto Rico.

The Foundation Center is an independent national service organization which provides an authoritative source of information on private philanthropic giving. It

offers a wide variety of services and comprehensive collections of information on foundations and grants in its
substantial reference collections located in New York
City, the District of Columbia, Cleveland, and San Francisco. In addition, the Center has established a "Cooperating Collections" network with libraries, community
foundations, and other nonprofit information centers located in every state and Puerto Rico. The Cooperating
Collections provide free public access to the Foundation
Center's core collection. The following publications comprise the Center's core collection:

- *The Foundation Directory, Parts 1 and 2*
- *The Foundation Directory Supplement*
- *The Foundation 1000*
- *Foundation Fundamentals*
- *Foundation Giving*
- *The Foundation Grants Index*
- *The Foundation Grants Index Quarterly*
- *Foundation Grants to Individuals*
- *Guide to U.S. Foundations, Their Trustees, Officers, and Donors*
- *The Foundation Center's Guide to Proposal Writing*
- *National Directory of Corporate Giving*
- *National Directory of Grantmaking Public Charities*
- *National Guide to Funding... (series)*
- *The Foundation Center's User–Friendly Guide*
- *The Foundation Center's Guide to Grantseeking on the Web*

To get the addresses, phone numbers, and operating
hours of each member of the Cooperating Collection network, visit URL http://www.fdncenter.org/collections/
index.html on the Internet. Most states have several Cooperating Collections.

Many Cooperating Collections offer, for public use,
sets of private foundation information returns (IRS
990-PF) for their state or region. You can see a complete

set of U.S. foundation returns at the Foundation Center's New York and Washington, D.C. Offices. Its Atlanta, Cleveland, and San Francisco offices have IRS Form 990–PF returns for the Southeastern, Midwestern, and Western states, respectively.

---

### FOUNDATION CENTER'S PRIMARY COLLECTIONS

The Foundation Center's primary collections are at:

## National Collection:

79 Fifth Ave.
New York, NY 10003
212/620–4230

### East Coast Collection:

Suite 938, 1001
Connecticut Ave., NW
Washington, DC 20036
202/331–1400

### Midwest Collection:

Kent H. Smith Library
Suite 1356, 1422 Euclid
Cleveland, OH 44115
216/861–1933

### Southern Collection:

Suite 150, 50 Hurt Plaza,
Atlanta, GA 30303
404/880–0094

### West Coast Collection:

3312 Sutter Street
San Francisco, CA 94108
415/397–0902

---

# ORGANIZATIONS

The following organizations are also sources of philanthropic information, albeit not as extensive as what the Foundation Center and its Cooperating Collections network offer. On the other hand, each of these groups can offer more detailed information on its specific field.

**AAFRC Trust for Philanthropy**
**American Association of Fund–Raising Council**
25 West 43rd St.
New York, NY 10036
212/354–5799

**American Council for the Arts**
1285 Avenue of the Americas
New York, NY 10018
212/245–4510

**American Council on Education**
Suite 800, 1 DuPont Circle
Washington, DC 20036
202/939–9300

**American Prospect Research Association**
Suite 905, 1600 Wilson Blvd.
Arlington, VA 22200
703/525–1191

**Association for Healthcare Philanthropy**
Suite 400, 313 Park Avenue
Falls Church, VA 22046
703/532–6243

**Business Committee for the Arts, Inc.**
1770 Broadway
New York, NY 10019
212/664–0600

**The Conference Board**
845 Third Avenue
New York, NY 10022
212/759–0900

## Council for Aid of Education
51 Madison Avenue
New York, NY 10010
212/689–2400

## Council for Advancement and Support of Education
Suite 400, 11 DuPont Circle, NW
Washington, DC 20036
202/328–5900

## Council of Jewish Federations
730 Broadway
New York, NY 10003
212/598–3500

## Council on Foundations
Suite 1200, 1828 L St., NW
Washington, DC 20036
202/466–6512

## Evangelical Council for Financial Accountability
P.O. Box 17456
Washington, DC 20041
703/435–8888

## Federation of Protest Welfare Agencies
281 Park Avenue South
New York, NY 10010
212/777–4800

## The Foundation Center
79 Fifth Avenue
New York, NY 10003
212/620–4230; toll–free: 800/424–9836

## Foundation for Independent Higher Education
Suite 218, 4 Landmark Square
Stamford, CT 06901
703/353–1544

## The Fund Raising School
Indiana University Center on Philanthropy
850 West Michigan St.
Indianapolis, IN 46223
317/274–4200

## Independent Sector
1828 L St., NW
Washington, DC 20036
202/223–8100

## Lutheran Resources Commission
5 Thomas Circle, NW
Washington, DC 20036
202/667–9844

## National Association of Independent Schools
18 Tremont St.
Boston, MA 02109
617/723–6900

## National Catholic Development Conference
86 Front St.
Hempstead, NY 11550
516/481–6000

## National Catholic Stewardship Council
1275 K St., NW
Washington, DC 20005
202/289–1093

## National Charities Information Bureau
19 Union Square West
New York, NY 10003
212/929–6300

### National Committee for Responsive Philanthropy
Suite 620, 2001 S St., NW
Washington, DC 20009
202/387–9177

### National Committee on Planned Giving
Indiana University Center on Philanthropy
550 West North St.
Indianapolis, IN 46202
317/684–8918

### National Council of Churches
Suite 868, 475 Riverside Dr.
New York, NY 10027
212/870–2511

### National Health Council
1700 K St. NW
Washington, DC 20006
202/785–3913

### National Society of Fund Raising Executives
Suite 3000, 1101 King St.
Alexandria, VA 22314
703/684–0410

### The National Volunteer Center
1111 North 19th St.
Arlington, VA 22209
703/276–0542

Chapter

12

# Resource Collection

Nobody in his right mind pretends that there is only one career book with all the answers for your transition to the nonprofit universe. While *From Making a Profit to Making a Difference: How to Launch Your New Career in Nonprofits* provides the guidance you need to make the transition from the business world to nonprofits, we've gathered together a number of very helpful resources to use with this book. We've chosen to tell you something about many of them to help you decide which ones will help you the most. You can get full descriptions of the other books listed by visiting our web site as described on the next page. We offer a free, complete *Job Quest Catalog* with over 400 career resources, both online and by mail. You can request it by any of the methods described on the next page or see it on our web site. *Please note that prices are subject to change without notice.*

## HOW TO ORDER

- [ ] **Toll–free phone at 888/366–5200** from within the United States, and at 708/366–5200 when calling from outside the U.S. Call us weekdays, between 9 a.m. and 6 p.m. Central Time.

- [ ] **Fax**. Complete the order form on page 177 (including credit card information) and fax it to 708/366–5280.

- [ ] **Email**. Simply supply the information requested on the order form on page 177 (including credit card information) and email it to: dl@jobfindersonline.com.

- [ ] **The Internet**. Visit our web site located at URL http://jobfindersonline.com where you'll find our *Job Quest Catalog Online* plus the latest free "Update Sheets" for all the *Job Finders* described on page 174.

- [ ] **Real world mail**. Send your prepaid order to:

Planning/Communications
Dept. FMP
7215 Oak Avenue
River Forest, IL 60305–1935

Should we ever move our offices, you can always find our new real world address by visiting our web site at: http://jobfindersonline.com

### 60–DAY RETURNS:

If you are dissatisfied with any item you purchase from this resource collection, call 708/366–5200 within 60 days of your shipping date to get a Return Merchandise Authorization (RMA) number and shipping instructions. Refunds of your purchase price are available only if the item is in new, sellable condition (no damage, no marks).

# FINDING JOB VACANCIES

### Non–Profits & Education Job Finder

Daniel Lauber, paperback $16.95, hard cover $32.95, 1997, 340 pages; free updates at http://jobfindersonline.com; will be replaced in late 2001 by two books, the *Nonprofits Job Finder* and the *Education Job Finder*

Get the scoop on over 2,222 reliable resources, both on-line and offline, where you'll find current job openings in the nonprofit sector, including job–hunting tools that get you hired: online Internet job and resume databases, job–listing periodicals, job–matching services, specialty and trade magazines, and job hotlines, plus directories of individuals for networking and directories of employers for "blind" job applications and researching potential employers. The salary surveys listed help you negotiate a higher salary. It's the perfect companion to the book that is now in your hands.

### Professional's Job Finder

Daniel Lauber, paperback $18.95, hard cover $32.95, 1997, 340 pages; free updates at http://jobfindersonline.com; succeeding editions in late 2001

If you'd rather find a job in health care or the private sector, this book presents complete details on over 3,003 job sources for positions in the private sector, including health care.

### Government Job Finder

Daniel Lauber, paperback $16.95, hard cover $32.95, 1997, 340 pages; free updates at http://jobfindersonline.com; next edition in late 2001

If government is your bag, this book offers the skinny on more than 2,002 job sources for local, state, and federal government — the only book of its kind!

### International Job Finder

Daniel Lauber, paperback $19.95, hard cover $32.95, available beginning August 2000, 192 pages; free updates at http://jobfindersonline.com

Put the world at your fingertips with details on over 1,001 online and offline sources of international jobs in the U.S. and abroad. This is where the Internet really shines.

### National Job Hotline Directory: The Job Finder's Hot List

Sue Cubbage and Marcia Williams, paperback $16.95, hard cover $32.95, 1999, 376 pages; free updates at http://jobfindersonline.com

Includes over 6,500 job hotlines on which companies, schools, and government agencies advertise job openings from CEO to sanitary engineer before they advertise them elsewhere. Organized by cities within each state.

# RESOURCES FOR NONPROFIT CAREERS

### Non–Profits & Education Job Finder

See the description on page 174.

### From Making a Profit to Making a Difference:
#### How to Launch Your New Career in Nonprofits

Richard King, $16.95 paperback, $29.95 hard cover, 2000,178 pages

This is the book you're holding in your hands.

### Jobs & Careers with Nonprofit Organizations

Ronald and Caryl Krannich, $17.95, 1999, 259 pages, 2nd edition

An ideal supplement to the book you're reading, it includes directories of over 300 domestic and global nonprofits; a test to determine if you have the right skills, motivations, and attitudes to thrive in the nonprofit world; a practical discussion of the negatives and positives of working for nonprofits, and an examination of the myths about working for nonprofits. Includes additional advice on conducting your nonprofit job search plus sample resumes and cover letters.

### The 100 Best Nonprofits to Work For

L. Hamilton and R. Tragert, $15.95, 1998, 282 pages

Profiles 100 of today's best paying, most secure, and most gratifying nonprofit organizations to work for. Each nonprofit is rated according to stability, career prospects, compensation, work environment, and pros and cons.

### Good Works: A Guide to Careers in Social Change

Jessica Colvin, editor, preface by Ralph Nader, $24.00, 1994, 682 pages

This humongous tome profiles over 1,000 nonprofits throughout the U.S. Each profile provides the essential information you need to decide if the group is right for you: its purpose, methods of operation, recent issues and projects, budget, funding sources, staff, staff openings a year, compensation, internships, where it advertises vacancies, to whom to apply. Includes geographic and topical indices.

*100 Jobs in Social Change*
Harley Jebens, $14.95, 216 pages
*Careers in Social Work*
Leon Ginsberg, $24.00, 246 pages
*Social Work Career Development*
Carol Nesslein Doelling, $24.95, 325 pages
*Curriculum Vita Handbook* — Anthony & Roe, $15.96, 166 pages
*JobBank Guide to Health Care Companies* — $17.95, 672 pages

## CHANGING CAREERS

*Directory of Executive Recruiters* — Kennedy Publications, $47.95, 1,361 pages
*What Color is Your Parachute?* — R. Bolles, $16.95, annual, 349 pages
*Change Your Job, Change Your Life* — R. Krannich, $17.95, 317 pages
*Zen and the Art of Making a Living* — L. Boldt, $17.95, 640 pages
*Discover What You're Best At* — Linda Gale, $13.00, 181 pages
*Career Tests* — Louis Janda, $12.95, 256 pages
*What Can You Do With a Law Degree? A Lawyer's Guide to Career Alternatives Inside, Outside, and Around the Law* — Deborah Arron, $29.95, 400 pages, 4th edition
*Flight Attendant Job Finder & Career Guide* — Kirkwood, $16.95, 178 pages

## APPLYING FOR THE JOB

*High Impact Resumes and Letters*
Dr. Ronald Krannich & William Banis, $19.95, 305 pages, 7th edition
*WinWay Resume Software* (Latest Version)
$52.46, you save 25% off the $69.95 retail price, CD–ROM, requires Windows 95 or higher to use the full program; includes Windows 3.1 version as well.
*Resumes for Re–Entry: A Handbook for Women* — Good, $10.95, 180 pages
*Resume Magic* — Susan Britton Whitcomb, $19.95, 596 pages
*Cyberspace Resume Kit* — Nemnich & Jandt, $16.95, 332 pages
*Electronic Resumes & Online Networking* — Smith, $13.99, 224 pages
*Dynamite Cover Letters* — Ron and Caryl Krannich, $14.95, 193 pages
*The Interview Rehearsal Book* — Gottesman & Mauro, $12.00, 128 pages
*Interview for Success* — Caryl & Ron Krannich, $15.95, 1998,pages
*Power Interviews: Job–Winning Tactics from Fortune 500 Recruiters* — Neil Yeager & Lee Hough, $14.95, 256 pages, revised edition

Please clearly print the title, price, quantity and
total for each different item ordered and follow the
instructions below. **Prepaid orders only**.

| Title or Kit | Price | x | Quantity | = | Total |
|---|---|---|---|---|---|
| _____ | $ __.__ | x | _____ | = | $ __.__ |
| _____ | $ __.__ | x | _____ | = | $ __.__ |
| _____ | $ __.__ | x | _____ | = | $ __.__ |
| _____ | $ __.__ | x | _____ | = | $ __.__ |
| _____ | $ __.__ | x | _____ | = | $ __.__ |
| _____ | $ __.__ | x | _____ | = | $ __.__ |
| _____ | $ __.__ | x | _____ | = | $ __.__ |
| _____ | $ __.__ | x | _____ | = | $ __.__ |
| _____ | $ __.__ | x | _____ | = | $ __.__ |
| _____ | $ __.__ | x | _____ | = | $ __.__ |

**Total Purchase:** $ __.__

**Add Shipping** ($5/first item + $1 each additional item): + $ 5.00

Additional items: _____ x $1 [Kits consist of 4 or 5 items] = $ __.__

If shipping to a destination outside the U.S., Canada, or U.S. military
addresses: Add an additional $14 per item (if postage is less, we
will send a refund of the difference to you with your books) + $ __.__

**Subtotal (Add the four shaded lines above)** = $ __.__

Illinois residents only → Add 7.75% sales tax + $ __.__

**Total Due** (Add the Subtotal and Sales Tax lines) = $ __.__

**Ordering instructions are on page 173.**

**SHIP TO:** **Please type or print clearly**.

Name _____

Address _____

_____
*Please supply a street address and apartment number so we can ship via UPS.*

City–State–Zip Code _____

Phone number _____ / _____ – _____ ❑ Home ❑ Work

Email address _____ FMP2000

❑ Enclosed is my check or money order for $ _____.___ (Total Due) payable
to "Planning/Communications."

❑ Please charge $ _____.___ (Total Due) to my VISA, MasterCard,
Discover Card, or American Express below:

Card # _____ Expiration date ___ / _____

Signature as on credit card _____

Photocopies of this form accepted

# About the Author

Having served in the nonprofit sector since 1969, author Richard King knows the nonprofit hiring process from both sides of the hiring desk. He is currently President of Kittleman and & Associates, LLC., one of the top executive search and management consulting firms that exclusively serve the nonprofit community nationwide. He joined Kittleman in 1985.

Mr. King has been the chief executive officer for three nonprofits: Wholistic Health Centers, Inc.; the Illinois Youth Service Bureau Association; and Youth in Crisis, Inc. He has served on boards of directors for several nonprofit organizations and consulted with dozens of nonprofits across the country on issues of governance, board development, long–range planning, fund raising, program development, and personnel appraisal.

Mr. King holds a Bachelor of Arts degree in Psychology from Illinois Wesleyan University, a Masters of Social Work from Florida State University, and a Masters of Business Administration with a concentration in Human Resources Administration from Dominican University. His academic background coupled with extensive experience managing and consulting with nonprofit organizations has provided him with a broad perspective on the dynamics of the management personnel selection process in the charitable sector.

A resident of Oak Park, Illinois, Mr. King was born in 1944 and grew up in Eureka, a small Central Illinois town. He and his wife Cheryl have two grown children, Megan and Cory.